D0599992

[ONLY IN BOOKS]

"Only in books has mankind known perfect truth, love and beauty."

GEORGE BERNARD SHAW

Only in BOOKS

Writers, Readers, & Bibliophiles on Their Passion

COMPILED BY
J. Kevin Graffagnino

MADISON HOUSE
Madison 1996

Graffagnino, J. Kevin
Only in Books
Writers, Readers, and Bibliophiles on Their Passion

LIBRARY OF CONGRESS CATALOGING-IN-PUBLICATION DATA

Only in books : writers, readers & bibliophiles on their passion /
compiled by J. Kevin Graffagnino.
p. cm.
Includes bibliographical references (p.) and index.
ISBN 0-945612-49-4 (alk. paper)
1. Books and reading—Quotations, maxims, etc.
2. Quotations, English. I. Graffagnino, J. Kevin.
PN6084.B65055 1996
002—dc20 96-26811
CIP

Designed and produced by
Impressions Book and Journal Services, Inc.
Madison, Wisconsin and Ann Arbor, Michigan

Printed in the United States of America on acid-free paper.
Published by Madison House Publishers, Inc.
P.O. Box 3100
Madison, Wisconsin 53704

FIRST EDITION

[CONTENTS]

For Gertrude R. Mallary
the finest bibliophile I know

[INTRODUCTION]

Confessions of an Unrepentant Bibliophile

In a June 10, 1815, letter to John Adams, Thomas Jefferson wrote, "I cannot live without books." That five-word statement by the man whose personal collection became the foundation of the Library of Congress expresses a feeling that has captured the hearts and minds of bookish individuals from Socrates to Swift to Styron. Whether they think of themselves as bibliophiles, avid readers, bibliofools, bookworms, bibliomaniacs, book collectors, or (to borrow Tom Raab's new term) biblioholics, men and women the world over have been falling under the spell of books for more than 2,000 years. For many the condition is a gentle hobby that involves little more than frequent reading and having hundreds of books around the house ("I know not how to abstain from reading," Samuel Pepys); for others it constitutes a serious, albeit pleasant drain on time, energy, space, and funds ("When we are collecting books, we are collecting happiness," Vincent Starrett); and for some it's an obsession in which the *need* to possess, hold, read, and immerse oneself in books becomes an irresistible passion ("People say that life is the thing, but I prefer reading," Logan Pearsall Smith). Even today, as we hurtle toward what some sadists describe as an all-electronic future of CD-ROMs, interactive video, distance learning, and the Internet, the traditional format of printed words on paper bound between two covers somehow retains substantial power to attract, fascinate, and satisfy.

As with most human passions, there is disagreement over whether booklovers are born or made. For my part, I can only say that I can't remember a time when I wasn't a bibliophile. I grew up surrounded by books. When I was a boy in Montpelier, Vermont, in the 1960s, our house contained somewhere around 1,000 books—then (and now, I suppose) considerably more than the average for an American home. My family's "library" was an eclectic, unplanned mix of subjects and titles. Thirty years later, I can remember concentrations in European and American history, dozens of beautifully printed Limited Editions Club volumes from the 1930s to the 1950s, various impressive but impenetrable classics from the Everyman Library series, and an assortment of modern literature, economics, biography, and philosophy. Even though there was almost nothing specifically aimed at children, beginning at about the age of nine or ten I still managed to fill many happy hours at home reading books I was too young to understand, plowing cover-to-cover through a near-complete run of *American Heritage*, and mining the tissue-thin pages of the eleventh edition of the *Encyclopædia Britannica* for arcane, out-of-date information to include in school papers and assignments. The absence of television—we were the only family I knew in Montpelier that didn't own a TV—may well have steered me toward books for entertainment, but I don't recall any particular sense of deprivation over having to substitute books for the delights of *My Three Sons*, *Bonanza* and *The Man from* U.N.C.L.E.

By far the most exciting books available to me at home were the remnants of the private library of Benjamin D. Silliman (1805–1901), a prominent nineteenth-century New York lawyer whose Manhattan real estate speculations produced a sizable fortune. Among the Silliman books that had traveled north from his Long Island estate to our house in Vermont were long eighteenth-century runs of the London monthly *Gentleman's Magazine*, early editions of world explorations, nineteenth-century natural-history titles, odd volumes from sets of the classics, signed presentation copies of popular travel narratives by such now-forgotten authors as George Coggeshall, and other examples of the reading material of a well-educated, intellectually curious Victorian gentleman of leisure. Silliman both read and annotated his books, and many of them bore pencil inscriptions detailing interesting meetings and conversations with such figures as Washington Irving and David Hosack, the doctor who treated Alexander Hamilton after his fatal duel with Aaron Burr. I can't recall *learning* much from poring over these antiquarian volumes with Silliman's "Scientia, Libertas et Virtus" bookplate, but I do remember that handling them filled me with a youthful sense of excitement and awe simply because they were old, mysterious, and wonderful. Although it didn't occur to me at the time, it must have been obvious to any adult watching me during those moments that I was a bookworm in the making.

Once begun, my bibliophilic evolution proceeded by fits and starts. At first, books had to compete with sports, in which I harbored powerful, seasonal aspirations of stardom in football, basketball, and baseball, with detours along the way for greatness in swimming, track and field, and cross-country running. It was fortunate for me that I also had books and reading, since those dreams of athletic glory never materialized, and gradually I concentrated more and more of my energy on bookish pursuits. At school I found that social studies, English, and history were the only areas in which I could excel without hard work, principally because I had an innate ability to read much faster than any of my classmates; in mathematics, the sciences, and all other subjects that required talents other than speed reading, I was content to achieve mere passing grades. A few Montpelier teachers, in particular Bonnie Merritt and Tom Benton, nurtured my one-sided interest. I still have the silver dollar Mrs. Merritt gave me in fifth grade for reading some 150 books during that school year, and the highlight of my eighth-grade existence (when the first of several serious knee injuries started me on an irreversible athletic decline) was the day I reached 3,600 words-per-minute in a reading test that Mr. Benton gave our class. Others in my grade may have eclipsed me on the playing fields or in the terrifying new world of adolescent dating, but at speed reading I was top gun and loudly triumphant about it.

My love of books took an antiquarian turn sometime in junior high school. I had already absorbed some of the bug from the Silliman books at home, and then around 1967 or 1968 I stumbled upon a copy of Van Allen Bradley's *Gold in Your Attic,* that popular guide to the monetary value of old books, at Montpelier's Kellogg-Hubbard Library. Reading Bradley took me out of coin collecting as a hobby and turned me into an eager young book scout certain I'd discover a pristine copy of Eliot's Indian Bible or the first edition of Poe's *Tamerlane* at some local yard sale or flea market—after all, Bradley said it could happen to anyone, so why not me? Liberal doses of the enthusiastic bibliophilic writings of A. E. Newton, William Dana Orcutt, and A. S. W. Rosenbach helped give that pipe dream more staying power than most of my teenage ambitions, and at seventeen I started a little used-book business I called "J. K. Graffagnino, Books." I hoped that a serious name would hide my utter lack of experience, knowledge, sale stock, and capital, and while I doubt whether I fooled anyone, most of the booklovers I encountered were too kind to point out my obvious shortcomings. After a few months of trying to buy and sell everything, regardless of subject or focus, I settled on Vermontiana as a specialty that was both manageable for me and popular with enough local collectors to allow some prospect of success. Eventually the business produced enough profit to pay my college bills, which was gratifying; still, it was the contact with books rather than the cash that was the real attraction. I'd probably have made more money mowing lawns or delivering pizzas like other impecunious undergraduates, but how many of them had a cramped apartment filled with dusty old tomes or could identify a first edition of *The Green Mountain Boys*? "After love," I'd read in Rosenbach, "book collecting is the most exhilarating sport of all," and I was happy in the knowledge that he was right.

J. K. Graffagnino, Books lasted for five years, until I reluctantly gave up the business to take a job in the Special Collections department of the University of Vermont library. In the nearly two decades since, most of my professional activity has revolved around caring for, writing about, learning from, and simply enjoying antiquarian Americana. If you count the teenage years as a bookseller, I've now spent more than half my life with books and libraries as the core of my existence. Like William Targ, when the time comes I'll be satisfied with the one-word epitaph, "Bookman," on my headstone. Having reached the age at which conventional wisdom says midlife crises and the realization that greatness lies out of reach make most of us ponder our choices in life, I've little sense of regret for the roads not taken. If there was another obsession calling, I never heard it; born or bred, I'm a bookman to the bone. For those of similar inclination, I heartily recommend it.

Wait a minute, I hear you say, is there really a future for books? The computer is king now: books will be forgotten soon, if in fact they're not already obsolete. In a few years we'll all be surfing the 'net, manipulating wireless mice to access interactive software, downloading unlimited digitized texts and pictures, and cruising the information superhighway. The complete works of Dickens are already available on CD-ROM; how long can it be before only a few fossilized bibliofools will have any use for words on paper? In another generation or so, books will be as anachronistic as slide rules, replaced by better, faster, and more exciting electronic formats. Librarians are now "information retrieval scientists"; little Johnny's computer literacy now worries his parents more than whether he can read and write; and Microsoft will lead us to a better future than any bibliofool ever envisioned. Books had a long run at the top, but it's over now.

Sorry, I don't buy it. Yes, computers are revolutionizing many aspects of our lives, and I'm no latter-day Luddite regarding them. It's been nearly a decade since I wrote anything except on a computer; I rely on my PC every day at work; I'm addicted to the convenience of e-mail; I know the advantages online library catalogs have over their paper predecessors; and I'm happy to welcome computers into any part of my professional or personal existence in which they're more useful than the other tools at my disposal. But the love of books isn't *about* work and tools. I'll gladly use a computerized encyclopedia or other reference title to find the facts I need; after all, much of "retrieving information" is drudgery, and I'm glad to be able to make it faster and easier. However, I don't think most people care about having *A Tale of Two Cities* on CD-ROM ("Or in any other format, for my money," one of my reading-challenged colleagues grumbled when she heard me voice that opinion) unless they're doing something like counting the number of times Jerry Cruncher appears in the text. For anyone who actually wants to read Dickens' timeless novel, there's no better way to do so than taking the book to a favorite chair and exercising your imagination from "It was the best of times; it was the worst of times" all the way to " 'It is a far better thing that I do, than I have ever done; it is a far, far better rest that I go to, than I have ever known.' " Dire predictions of the end of books and reading have been with us for nearly a century, but their staying power against the challenges of movies, radio, and television makes me confident they'll still have a prominent place in the computer age as well.

Nearly forty years ago, Lawrence Clark Powell, one of this country's most eloquent bibliophiles, wrote in *A Passion for Books,* "I believe that books—those beautiful blends of form and spirit—have a future fully as glorious as their past." I'm with Powell on that one, and like him, I'm certain "that I am not alone in my belief, my faith, my love." The bookstores I visit are always crowded; everywhere I go I see people reading just for the pleasure of it; the libraries I frequent are busy, bustling places; in short, the love of old and new books alike seems to be thriving as we near the end of the twentieth century. I don't claim to be able to explain the allure of reading, the appeal of a signed first edition, or the magic of a Civil War soldier's letter in its original envelope, any more than I can explain why a monarch butterfly is beautiful, but I know the power of those bookish attractions for me and those like me. There are enough avid bibliofools for whom the love of reading is a constant, irresistible fact of life that I'm not worried about having "computer" become the penultimate word in "I'm going to curl up with a good book tonight." Yes, there are many barbarians at the gate, unfortunate wretches who fail to see the light; but they have always been with us, and to deal with them, in Powell's words, "I call on booklovers everywhere to close ranks, face the invaders, and give them the works, preferably in elephant folio."

This project of compiling quotes about books and reading into a published collection had its beginnings more than twenty years ago. I started accumulating bookish sayings as a teenager in the early 1970s and have kept at it more or less ever since. The first two quotations that I can recall writing down and taping to the wall above my desk were Desiderius Erasmus' familiar reflection on buying books instead of food and clothes and Thomas Sheridan's quatrain declaring time spent with books preferable to "conversing with lords and dukes." Quote hunting remained an occasional pastime for the next two decades, as I gathered possibilities from my own reading, the booklovers' musings that often graced the front cover of *Antiquarian Bookman's Weekly*, Bartlett's and other standard quotation collections, submissions by helpful friends and colleagues, anthologies of bibliophilic writings, and a variety of other sources. At the outset, I concentrated mainly on quotes about antiquarian books, but in time my horizons widened to include interesting observations on libraries, reading, book design and production, history, biography, authorship, and the significance of printing. When I moved from Vermont to the Midwest last year to become Library Director at the State Historical Society of Wisconsin, I decided to devote more time to the quotes project as a way of ensuring that sinking to the level of full-time administrator wouldn't keep me from ever having contact with books again. That strategy has worked so far, but now that I'm done with this undertaking I'm worried about a future in which meetings, management, and memoranda will crowd out more congenial and satisfying pursuits.

As the job of imposing order on a haphazard jumble of handwritten slips and cards proceeded, I was pleasantly surprised by how many good bibliophilic quotations I'd managed to find over the years. I knew I'd found fertile ground in the writings of such leaders of the literary canon as Chaucer, Shakespeare, and Milton, and I remembered writing down favorite sayings while reading Newton, Richard de Bury, Thomas F. Dibdin, Rosenbach, and Orcutt, but I hadn't realized how many other authors had made their way into my files. Skimming the typescript from A to E, I see entries for Addison, Austen, Byron, Carlyle, Cervantes, Cicero, Clemens, Coleridge, Dickens, Dickinson, Eliot, and Emerson among the "big name" authors, along with dozens of pithy quotes by less famous librarians (Randolph G. Adams, Fredson Bowers, Melvil Dewey), writers (Bronson Alcott, Ambrose Bierce, Samuel Butler, G. K. Chesterton, William Congreve), collectors (Augustine Birrell, Reginald A. Brewer, Barton W. Currie), and numerous "others." There's something of a pecking order to who got in and who didn't: Shakespeare qualifies with "Come, and take choice of all my library;/ And so beguile thy sorrow," but Arnold Louis Maurice Seguier had to come up with something short, sweet, and memorable ("If someone wishes to seduce me, he has only to offer me books") to gain inclusion. In order to keep the collection to a manageable length, authors who have written extensively and charmingly on books (Dibdin, Newton, de Bury, William Hazlitt, Rosenbach, Powell, Vincent Starrett) got a representative selection of their "best" rather than pages and pages of fair-to-middling entries.

The arrangement of this volume is alphabetical by author, which I found resulted in a chronological and topical variety that appealed more to me than grouping the quotes by subject or date. Nonetheless, readers who dip into this volume will find that the contents do break down into a handful of large subject blocs. There are dozens of quotations about the joys of reading, from Leo Allatius ("To me, the light of the sun, the day, and life itself, would be joyless and bitter if I had not something to read") to Eudora Welty ("I learned from the age of two or three that any room in our house, at any time of day, was there to read in, or to be read to"). Most of these correctly extol reading as the point of human existence ("If I couldn't read, I couldn't live," Thelma Green), but a few fall short of true enlightenment ("Books are good enough in their own way, but they are a mighty bloodless substitute for life," Robert Louis Stevenson). The travails of authorship get ample coverage, particularly from writers detailing the burdens of their profession ("There's nothing to writing. All you do is sit down at the typewriter and open a vein," Red Smith) and the evil nature of publishers ("Now Barabbas was a publisher," Thomas Campbell) and reviewers ("Beat him to death, the dog! He's a reviewer!," J. W. Goethe). The flip side of that coin turns up less frequently but with considerable effect in withering estimations of writers by their allies and enemies in the production of books ("Many authors should be shunned socially. Some are almost not human," William Targ). My favorites in this category are those quotes in which one eminent writer presents an unflattering opinion of another; for particularly memorable entries along those lines, see Clemens on Austen, Coleridge on Gibbon, James on Poe, Shaw on Shakespeare, Tennyson on Jonson, and Wilde on James.

Because my college degrees are in History, and since I share Samuel Johnson's inclination toward biography, there are many quotations in both fields included here. Like Bertrand Russell, I've put off writing my autobiography "for fear of something important having not yet happened," but I'm intrigued by what so many fellow biographers and historians have had to say about our craft, and by how unfavorably the rest of the world seems to perceive us. If we are to believe the authors before us in this volume, biography and history consist mostly of lies, half-truths, and indifferent prose. Bad enough that Ambrose Bierce defines history as "An account mostly false, of events mostly unimportant, which are brought about by rulers mostly knaves, and soldiers mostly fools"; at least there more of the blame seems to fall on those who make history than on those who write it. It's considerably more difficult to put a good face on Johnson's "Great abilities are not requisite for an historian, for in historical composition all the greatest powers of the human mind are quiescent," much less Shaw's " 'History, sir, will tell lies, as usual.' " Thank the book gods for Oscar Wilde, one of my favorite sources of wonderful quotations, who reminds us that "Anyone can make history. Only a great man can write it."

Yet, while history is where my personal research and reading interests lie, I've drawn my paycheck the past two decades from library work, and thus I've also succumbed to the impulse to sprinkle quotations about libraries and librarians throughout this collection. I applaud the discernment of Augustine Birrell ("A great library easily begets affection, which may deepen into love"), and I'd gladly pay to have the wise observations of Charles Kendall Adams ("In every University of character, the library is regarded as of fundamental importance") and Shelby Foote ("A university is just a group of buildings gathered around a library") engraved in Gothic letters on the granite foreheads of college and university administrators nationwide. If there's any money left over, I'll spring for tattoos drawn from C. Waller Barrett ("If the library is the heart of the university, the rare book area is the heart of the library") and Fredson Bowers ("That five hundred may busy themselves in the general collection for the one who reads in the rare-book room means little when quality, not quantity, is the criterion") for all academic librarians who think of themselves as "informational media specialists" and dream of abolishing their special collections departments. Browsing through this volume will acquaint readers with other perspectives on libraries, including sentimental recollections of their positive impact on individual lives, numerous (and occasionally stuffy) statements about their importance to society and their future in the electronic age, excerpts from novels with library settings, and whimsical observations (cf. Edmund L. Pearson, in particular) on the general public's perception of library work and the men and women who do it. Apart from some regrettable outright falsehoods ("It is not observed that . . . librarians are wiser than other men," Ralph Waldo Emerson), I hope that the entries in this category will nurture faith in the enticing vision of Jorge Luis Borges "that Paradise will be a kind of library."

In the end, though, my favorite category in this collection comes full circle to the quotations linking the love of reading and the antiquarian impulses that Benjamin D. Silliman's books and *Gold in Your Attic* first awakened in me some thirty years ago. Throughout this volume there are quotes that speak to the dual passion for reading and old books that has shaped my life. While my bibliomania has not yet advanced quite so far as Eugene Field's ("If I know one thing better than another I know this, that my books know me and love me"), still I know how Jefferson felt, and I agree with Theodore C. Blegen that "the human impulse to collect reaches one of its highest levels in the domain of books." I've long since given up any qualms about being a clone of Virginia Woolf's "bookish man" (even though I don't own a dressing gown) or spending my time "gloating on the musty page" in imitation of Royall Tyler's bookworm. Like Southey, "I am frankly a little mad about books," and I'm long past caring who knows it. Membership in a group that includes such past and present bibliofools as de Bury, Rosenbach, Newton, Starrett, Powell, and Targ suits me perfectly; after all, as Robert M. Williamson wrote nearly a century ago, "In all ages the greatest, best, and most lovable men have been lovers of books." Driven as I am by these twin infatuations, I'll make more allowances than Rosenbach for people ("I've been told there are intelligent people") who value handsome modern books as much as first editions in original boards. Whether the volumes in question are old or new, it's enough for me that my friends demonstrate a profound belief in Newton's great truth, "The buying of more books than one can read is nothing less than the soul reaching toward infinity, and this passion is the only thing that raises us above the beasts that perish." Anyone who understands that should find something of interest in this little collection.

[ACKNOWLEDGMENTS]

BECAUSE THIS PROJECT of gathering bookish quotations has stretched over a quarter-century, I am indebted to many individuals for supplying quotes, leads, references, and other support. The constraints of space and memory prevent my listing every individual who has contributed to this work, but I do want to thank the colleagues, friends, and acquaintances who have been most helpful. At the University of Vermont, where I studied and worked for more than twenty years, I received inspiration and assistance from John Buechler, Connell Gallagher, Jeffrey Marshall, Karen Stites Campbell, Sam Hand, Harry Orth, and Betty Bandel, among others. Other Vermonters who lent a hand from time to time include Frances L. Robinson, J. Robert Maguire, George Singer, Rocky Stinehour, Ida Washington, Michael Sherman, Peter Mallary, Nancy Spencer, John McSweeney, Ray Maloney, Robert A. Sharp, and William L. Parkinson.

Bibliomania is not strictly a Green Mountain affliction, however, and many people from "away" also deserve my appreciation. In Wisconsin, where this book evolved during the past year from a mass of unorganized quotations to a published volume, I benefited from the interest and participation of Bill Bessler, Bill Cronon, Greg Britton, John Kaminski, Jim Danky, Rich Leffler, Dean Connors, Michael Edmonds, Ken Frazier, Bill Kasdorf, Wayne Wiegand, and Nick Muller. Among the fellow bibliophiles not fortunate enough to live in Vermont or Wisconsin but who also contributed are Calvin P. Otto, Marcus A. McCorison, Myrtle Lane, and Norman Stevens. As always, the individual to whom my greatest thanks are due is my wife and most-valued colleague Leslie A. Hasker, who for twenty years has displayed a rare grace in tolerating a husband who converses largely in quotations and each day grows more like the dusty fellow on the ladder in Carl Spitzweg's "The Bookworm."

Finally, I want to thank the following authors and publishers for permission to use quotations from copyrighted titles:

Lawrence Clark Powell, for material from his works *The Alchemy of Books* (Los Angeles, 1954) and *A Passion For Books* (Cleveland, 1958); Stuart Brent, for several quotations from *The Seven Stairs* (1962; reprint ed., New York, 1989); Don Congdon Associates, Inc., for a passage from Ray Bradbury, *The Martian Chronicles* (Garden City, N.Y., 1950); Simon & Schuster, for material from *How to Read a Book* by Mortimer J. Adler and Charles Van Doren, copyright 1972 by Mortimer J. Adler and Charles Van Doren; Prometheus Books, for a quotation from Eric Burns, *The Joy of Books: Confessions of a Lifelong Reader* (Amherst, N.Y., 1995); Thomas R. Brewer, for a passage from Reginald A. Brewer, *The Delightful Diversion: The Whys and Wherefores of Book Collecting* (New York, 1935); Random House, Inc., for material from Truman Capote, *Breakfast at Tiffany's* (New York, 1958); Houghton Mifflin Company, for excerpt from *Yankee Bookseller* by Charles E. Goodspeed, copyright 1937 by Charles E. Goodspeed, renewed 1965 by Charles T. Goodspeed, and reprinted by permission of Houghton Mifflin Company, all rights reserved; Harvard University Press, for quotations from *Writing was Everything* by Alfred Kazin, copyright 1995 by Alfred Kazin, reprinted by permission of Harvard University Press; State House Press, for a passage from James Michener, *Literary Reflections: Michener on Michener, Hemingway, Capote, and Others* (Austin, Tex., 1993); Estate of Edna Ferber, for excerpts from *A Kind of Magic* (Garden City, N.Y., 1963); Ronald Randall, for a quotation from David A. Randall, *Dukedom Large Enough* (New York, 1969); Harcourt Brace & Company, for excerpts from *The Human Comedy*, copyright 1943 and renewed 1971 by William Saroyan, reprinted by permission of Harcourt Brace & Company; The Bookpress, for material from E. Millicent Sowerby, *Rare Books and Rare People* (1967; reprint ed., Williamsburg, Va., 1987); University of Oklahoma Press, for quotations from Vincent Starrett, *Born in a Bookshop: Chapters from the Chicago Renascence* (Norman, Ok., 1965), copyright 1965 by the University of Oklahoma Press, Publishing Division of the University; Scribner, a division of Simon & Schuster, for a passage from *Of Time and the River* by Thomas Wolfe; copyright 1935 by Charles Scribner's Sons, renewed 1963 by Paul Gitlin, Administrator C. T. A.; Farrar, Straus and Giroux, for excerpt from Isaac Bashevis Singer, *Enemies, a Love Story* (New York, 1972); Little, Brown & Company, for selections from Barton W. Currie, *Fishers of Books* (Boston, 1931); Little, Brown & Company, for material from A. S. W. Rosenbach, *Books and Bidders* (Boston, 1927); William Targ, for quotations from *Indecent Pleasures: The Life and Colorful Times of William Targ* (New York, 1975), reprinted by permission of the Roslyn Targ Literary Agency, Inc., copyright 1975 by William Targ.

The illustrations in this volume are selected examples of late nineteenth- and early twentieth-century American book-plates.

[ONLY IN BOOKS]

Herbert
Spencer
Allen
His
Book
Frederick
Garrison
J. Winfred
Spenceley
Sc. 1903

CHARLES KENDALL ADAMS
1835–1902

"In every University of character, the library is regarded as of fundamental importance."

FRANKLIN P. ADAMS
1881–1960

"Having imagination, it takes you an hour to write a paragraph that, if you were unimaginative, would take only a minute. Or you might not write the paragraph at all."

"The best part of the fiction in many novels is the notice that the characters are all purely imaginary."

HENRY ADAMS
1838–1918

"Books remained as in the eighteenth century, the source of life, and as they came out—Thackeray, Dickens, Bulwer, Tennyson, Macaulay, Carlyle, and the rest—they were devoured, but as far as happiness went, the happiest hours of the boy's education were passed in summer lying on a musty heap of Congressional Documents in the old farmhouse at Quincy, reading 'Quentin Durward,' 'Ivanhoe,' and 'The Talisman,' and raiding the garden at intervals for peaches and pears. On the whole he learned most then."

JOHN ADAMS
1735–1826

"My Friends or Enemies continue to overwhelm me with Books. Whatever may be their intension, charitable or otherwise, they certainly contribute, to continue me to vegetate, much as I have done for the sixteen Years last past."

"This wandering, itinerating Life grows more and more disagreeable to me. I want to see my Wife and Children every Day, I want to see my Grass and Blossoms and Corn, &c. every Day. I want to see my Workmen. . . . But above all except the Wife and Children I want to see my Books."

JOHN QUINCY ADAMS
1767–1848

"There is such seduction in a library of good books that I cannot resist the temptation to luxuriate in reading."

RANDOLPH G. ADAMS
1892–1951

"Book collecting and the building-up of great libraries is as much a matter of the heart as a matter of the head. The man who is all heart and no head would be a very bad librarian. But the man who is all head and no heart is a very dangerous librarian."

JOSEPH ADDISON
1672–1719

"Books are the legacies that genius leaves to mankind, to be delivered down from generation to generation, as presents to those that are yet unborn."

"Were all books reduced thus to their quintessence, many a bulky author would make his appearance in a pennypaper. There would be scarce such a thing in nature as a folio; the works of an age would be contained on a few shelves: not to mention millions of volumes that would be utterly annihilated."

"A reader seldom peruses a book with pleasure until he knows whether the writer of it be a black man or a fair man, of a mild or choleric disposition, married or a bachelor."

MORTIMER J. ADLER
1902–

". . . I have written a book about reading. Those who write about sex, or money-making, often give the impression that it is the whole of life. I do not want to give a similar impression about reading, but I do want to persuade you that it is a substantial part of the life of reason."

"However good reading may be as an immediate source of pleasure, it is not completely an end in itself. We must do more than think and learn in order to lead a human life. We must act. If we wish to preserve our leisure for disinterested activities, we cannot shirk our practical responsibilities. It is in relation to our practical life that reading has its ultimate justification."

HENRY CORNELIUS AGRIPPA VON NETTESHEIM
1486?–1535

"Historiographers disagree mightily among themselves and write such variable and different things about one event that it is impossible that a number of them should not be liars."

JOHN AIKEN
1747–1822

"The time to read is any time; no apparatus, no appointment of time and place, is necessary."

A. BRONSON ALCOTT
1799–1888

"Good books, like good friends, are few and chosen; the more select the more enjoyable; and like these are approached with diffidence, nor sought too familarily nor too often, having precedence only when friends tire."

"That is a good book which is opened with expectation and closed with profit."

"Books are the most mannerly of companions, accessible at all times, in all moods, frankly declaring the author's mind, without offence."

"The richest minds need not large libraries."

"One cannot celebrate books sufficiently. After saying his best, still something remains to be spoken in their praise."

LOUISA MAY ALCOTT
1832–1888

"She is too fond of books, and it has turned her brain."

"Love scenes, if genuine, are indescribable; for to those who have enacted them the most elaborate description seems tame, and to those who have not, the simplest pictures seems overdone."

"All is fish that comes to the literary net. Goethe puts his joys and sorrows into poems, I turn my adventures into bread and butter."

THOMAS BAILEY ALDRICH
1836–1907

"Books that have become classics—books that have had their day and now get more praise than perusal—always remind me of retired colonels and majors and captains who, having reached the age limit, find themselves retired on half-pay."

SHOLEM ALEICHEM
1859–1916

" . . . writing an autobiography and making a spiritual will are practically the same."

LEO ALLATIUS
1586–1669

"To me, the light of the sun, the day, and life itself, would be joyless and bitter if I had not something to read."

FRED ALLEN
1894–1956

"I can't understand why a person will take a year or two to write a novel when he can easily buy one for a few dollars."

WOODY ALLEN
1935–

"I remember when I was a little boy I once stole a pornographic book that was printed in Braille. And I used to rub the dirty parts."

KINGSLEY AMIS
1922–

"I'm always in a dither when starting a novel—that's the worst time. It's like going to the dentist, because you do make an appointment with yourself."

MARGARET ANDERSON
1893–1973

"It is rarely that you see an American author who is not hopelessly sane."

MAYA ANGELOU
1928–

"I had a large vocabulary and had been reading constantly since childhood, I had taken words and the art of arranging them."

THOMAS AQUINAS
1225?–1274

"I am a man of one book."

ARISTOTLE
384–322 B.C.

"To write well, express yourself like the common people, but think like a wise man."

"Poetry is more philosophical and of higher value than history."

MATTHEW ARNOLD
1822–1888

"A man's life each day depends for its solidity and value on whether he reads during that day, and, far more still, on what he reads during it."

THOMAS ARNOLD
1793–1842

"Preserve proportion in reading. Keep your view of men and things extensive."

SHOLEM ASCH
1880–1957

"Writing comes more easily if you have something to say."

ROGER ASCHAM
1515–1568

"My book hath been so much my pleasure, and bringeth daily to me more pleasure and more, that in respect of it, all pleasure in very deed be but trifles and troubles unto me."

W. H. AUDEN
1907–1973

"In the eyes of every author, I fancy, his own past work falls into four classes. First, the pure rubbish which he regrets ever having conceived; second—for him the most painful—the good ideas which his incompetence or impatience prevented from coming to much; third, the pieces he has nothing against except their lack of importance; these must inevitably form the bulk of any collection since, were he to limit it to the fourth class alone, to those poems for which he is honestly grateful, his volume would be too depressingly slim."

"Indeed there are few better ways of spending a hilarious evening than in recalling the worst lines in English poetry."

"No poet or novelist wishes he was the only one who ever lived, but most of them wish they were the only one alive, and quite a number fondly believe their wish has been granted."

"In our age if a boy or girl is untalented, the odds are in favour of their thinking they want to write."

"The girl whose boy-friend starts writing her love poems should be on her guard."

"Writing reviews can be fun, but I don't think the practice is very good for the character."

"But if a stranger in the train asks me for my occupation I never answer 'writer' for fear that he may go on to ask what I write, and to answer 'poetry' would embarrass us both, for we both know that nobody can earn a living simply by writing poetry."

"One cannot review a bad book without showing off."

SAINT AUGUSTINE
354–430

"Take up and read, take up and read."

MARCUS AURELIUS
121–180

"Away with thy books! Be no longer drawn aside by them: it is not allowed."

JANE AUSTEN
1775–1817

"I think I may boast myself to be, with all possible vanity, the most unlearned and uninformed female who ever dared to be an authoress."

" 'What are you reading, Miss ______?' 'Oh! it's only a novel!' replies the young lady; while she lays down her book with affected indifference, or momentary shame. . . . only some work in which the greatest powers of the mind are displayed; in which the most thorough knowledge of human nature, the happiest delineation of its varieties, the liveliest effusions of wit or humour, are conveyed to the world in the best chosen language."

" ' . . . I do not think I ever opened a book in my life which had not something to say upon woman's inconstancy. Songs and proverbs all talk of woman's fickleness. But, perhaps, you will say, these were all written by men.'

'Perhaps I shall. Yes, yes, if you please, no references to examples in books . . . the pen has been in their hands. I will not allow books to prove anything.' "

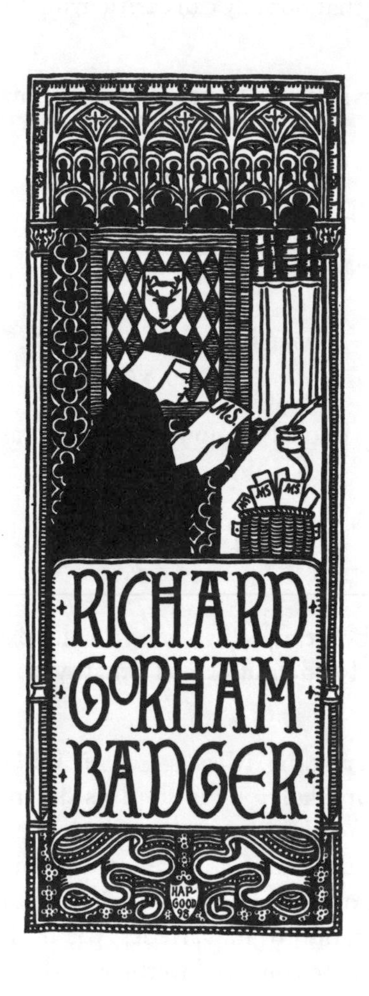
MS.
RICHARD
GORHAM
BADGER
HAP-
GOOD
98

FRANCIS BACON
1561–1626

"The reading of a good book serves for delight, for ornament, for ability. The crafty contemn it; the simple admire it; the wise use it."

"Some books are to be tasted, others to be swallowed, and some few to be chewed and digested; that is, some are to be read only in parts, others to be read but not curiously; and some few to be read wholly, and with diligence and attention. Some books may also be read by deputy, and extracts made of them by others."

"I have rather studied books than men."

"The multitude of books produces a deceitful impression of superfluity. This, however, is not to be remedied by destroying the books already written, but by making more good ones, which, like the serpent of Moses, may devour the serpents of the enchanters."

"The images of men's wits and knowledges remain in books, exempted from the wrong of time, and capable of perpetual renovation."

"Books will speak plain when counsellors blanch."

"Books must follow sciences, and not sciences books."

"So let great authors have their due, as time, which is the author of authors, be not deprived of his due, which is further and further to discover truth."

"Libraries, which are as the shrines where all the relics of the ancient saints, full of true virtue, and that without delusion or imposture, are preserved and reposed."

"Histories make men wise; poets, witty; the mathematics, subtile; natural philosophy, deep; morals, grave; logic and rhetoric, able to contend."

WALTER BAGEHOT
1826–1877

"Writers, like teeth, are divided into incisors and grinders."

"The reason why so few good books are written is that so few people that can write know anything."

"Superficial the reading of grown men in some sort must ever be; it is only once in a lifetime that we can know the passionate reading of youth."

RUSSELL BAKER
1925–

"Americans like fat books and thin women."

JAMES BALDWIN
1924–1987

". . . the Public Library, a building filled with books and unimaginably vast, and which he had never yet dared to enter . . . he had never gone in because the building was so big that it must be full of corridors and marble steps, in the maze of which he would be lost and never find the book he wanted."

"I started reading. I read everything I could get my hands on, murder mysteries, *The Good Earth*, everything. By the time I was thirteen I had read myself out of Harlem. I had read every book in two libraries and had a card for the Forty-Second Street branch."

"The writer's greed is appalling. He wants, or seems to want, everything and practically everybody; in another sense, and at the same time, he needs no one at all."

"You think your pains and your heartbreaks are unprecedented in the history of the world, but then you read. It was books that taught me that the things that tormented me most were the very things that connected me with all the people who were alive, or who have ever been alive."

ARTHUR JAMES BALFOUR
1848–1930

"He has only half learned the art of reading who has not added to it the more refined art of skipping and skimming."

"The world may be kind or unkind, it may seem to us to be hastening on the wings of enlightenment and progress to an imminent millenium, or it may weigh us down with the sense of insoluble difficulty and irremediable wrong; but whatever else it be, so long as we have good health and a good library, it can hardly be dull."

"There is no mood to which a man may not administer the appropriate medicine at the cost of reaching down a volume from his bookshelf."

"History does not repeat itself. Historians repeat each other."

"Biography should be written by an acute enemy."

HONORÉ DE BALZAC
1799–1850

"It is as easy to dream a book as it is hard to write one."

TONI CADE BAMBARA
1939–

"The story is a piece of work. The novel is a way of life."

MARGARET CULKIN BANNING
1891–1982

"Fiction is not a dream. Nor is it guesswork. It is imagining based on facts, and the facts must be accurate or the work of imagining will not stand up."

WILLIAM BARNES
1801–1886

"Books that purify the thought,
Spirits of the learned dead,
Teachers of the little taught,
Comforters when friends are fled."

C. WALLER BARRETT
1901–1991

"If the library is the heart of the university, the rare book room is the heart of the library."

JAMES M. BARRIE
1860–1937

"Times have changed since a certain author was executed for murdering his publisher. They say that when the author was on the scaffold he said goodbye to the minister and to the reporters, and then he saw some publishers sitting in the front row below, and to them he did not say goodbye. He said instead, 'I'll see you again.'"

"The printing-press is either the greatest blessing or the greatest curse of modern times, one sometimes forgets which."

"For several days after my first book was published I carried it about in my pocket, and took surreptitious peeps at it to make sure the ink had not faded."

THOMAS V. BARTHOLIN
1619–1680

"Without books, God is silent, justice dormant, natural science at a stand, philosophy lame, letters dumb, and all things involved in darkness."

CHARLES BAUDELAIRE
1821–1867

"Books bored me to death. I am disgusted with all that; only Victor Hugo's theatre and poetry and a book by Sainte-Beuve gave me any pleasure. I am absolutely fed up with literature."

"On the day when a young writer corrects his first proof-sheet he is as proud as a schoolboy who has just got his first dose of the pox."

RICHARD BAXTER
1615–1691

"It is not the reading of many books which is necessary to make a man wise or good, but the well-reading of a few, could he be sure to have the best."

PIERRE BAYLE
1641–1706

"If an historian were to relate truthfully all the crimes, weaknesses and disorders of mankind, his readers would take his work for satire rather than for history."

MARTHA BAYLES
1948–

"If we are told of some four-volume epic . . . we're apt to say 'How interesting,' but we never will read it unless we have both legs in traction."

SYLVIA BEACH
1887–1962

"Fitting people with books is about as difficult as fitting them with shoes."

"I think Hemingway's [book] titles should be awarded first prize in any contest. Each of them is a poem, and their mysterious power over readers contributes to Hemingway's success. His titles have a life of their own, and they have enriched the American vocabulary."

MARY RITTER BEARD
1876–1958

"Could anyone fail to be depressed by a book he or she has published? Don't we always outgrow them the moment the last page has been written?"

JAMES BEATTIE
1735–1803

"People read for amusement. If a book be capable of yielding amusement, it will naturally be read; for no man is an enemy to what gives him pleasure. Some books, indeed, being calculated for the intellects of a few, can please only a few; yet, if they produce this effect, they answer all the end the authors intended; and if those few be men of any note, which is generally the case, the herd of mankind will very willingly fall in with their judgment, and consent to admire what they do not understand."

SIMONE DE BEAUVOIR
1908–1986

"A woman writer is first a writer who consecrates her life to writing and has no other occupation."

"The writer of originality, unless dead, is always shocking, scandalous; novelty disturbs and repels."

HENRY WARD BEECHER
1813–1887

"No man has a right to bring up his children without surrounding them with good books if he has the means to buy them. A library is one of the necessities of life. A book is better for weariness than sleep; better for cheerfulness than wine; it is often a better physician than a doctor, and a better preacher than a minister."

"Let us pity those poor rich men who live barrenly in great bookless houses! Let us congratulate the poor that, in our day, books are so cheap that a man may every year add a hundred volumes to his library for the price of what his tobacco and beer would cost him. Among the earliest ambitions to be excited in clerks, workmen, journeymen, and, indeed, among all that are struggling up from nothing to something, is that of owning, and constantly adding to a library of good books. A little library, growing larger every year, is an honorable part of a young man's history. It is a man's duty to have books. A library is not a luxury, but one of the necessaries of life."

"Alas! Where is human nature so weak as in a bookstore? Speak of the appetite for drink; or of a bon-vivant's relish for a dinner! What are these mere animal throes and ragings compared with those fantasies of taste, of those yearnings of the imagination, of those insatiable appetites of intellect, which bewilder a student in a great book-seller's temptation-hall?"

"Moreover, buying books before you can pay for them, promotes caution. You do not feel quite at liberty to take them home. You are married. Your wife keeps an account-book. She knows to a penny what you can and what you can not afford. She has no 'speculation' in her eyes. Plain figures make desperate work with airy 'Somehows.' It is a matter of no small skill and experience to get your books home, and into their proper places undiscovered. Perhaps the blundering Express brings them to the door just at evening. 'What is it, my dear?' she says to you. 'Oh! nothing—a few books that I can not do without.' That smile! A true housewife that loves her husband, can smile a whole arithmetic at him in one look! Of course she insists, in the kindest way, in sympathizing with you in your literary acquisition. She cuts the strings of the bundle and of your heart, and out comes the whole story. You have bought a complete set of costly English books, full bound in calf, extra gilt. You are caught, and feel very much as if bound in calf yourself, and admirably lettered."

"A library is but the soul's burying ground. It is a land of shadows."

"How easily one may distinguish a genuine lover of books from the worldly man! With what subdued and yet glowing enthusiasm does he gaze upon the costly front of a thousand embattled volumes! How gently he draws them down, as if they were little children; how tenderly he handles them! He peers at the title-page, at the text, or the notes, with the nicety of a bird examining a flower. He studies the binding: the leather—Russia, English calf, morocco; the lettering, the gilding, the edging, the hinge of the cover! He opens it, and shuts it, he holds it off, and brings it nigh. It suffuses his whole body with book-magnetism."

"No subtle manager or broker ever saw through a maze of financial embarrassments half so quick as a poor book-buyer sees his way clear to pay for what he *must* have. He promises with himself marvels of retrenchment; he will eat less, or less costly viands, that he may buy food for the mind. He will take an extra patch, and go on with his raiment another year, and buy books instead of coats. He will lecture, teach, trade; he will do any honest thing for money to buy books!"

BRENDAN BEHAN
1923–1964

"An author's first duty is to let down his country."

ARTHUR W. BELL
1875–1945

"The test of real fame in literature is to be reprinted in the *Old Farmer's Almanac.*"

HILAIRE BELLOC
1870–1953

"When I am dead, I hope it may be said:
'His sins were scarlet, but his books were read.' "

"Child! do not throw this book about;
Refrain from the unholy pleasure
Of cutting all the pictures out!
Preserve it as your chiefest treasure."

"Just as there is nothing between the admirable omelette and the intolerable, so with autobiography."

SAUL BELLOW
1915–

"No wonder the really powerful men in our society, whether politicians or scientists, hold writers and poets in contempt. They do it because they get no evidence from modern literature that anybody is thinking about any significant question."

"A novel is balanced between a few true impressions and the multitude of false ones that make up most of what we call life."

"With a novelist, like a surgeon, you have to get a feeling that you've fallen into good hands—someone from whom you can accept the anesthetic with confidence."

STEPHEN VINCENT BENÉT
1898–1943

"Books are not men and yet they are alive,
They are man's memory and his aspiration,
The link between his present and his past,
The tools he builds with."

ARNOLD BENNETT
1867–1931

"A publisher must accustom the public to the spectacle of many books. If a bookshop displayed only the few really good books that get published in a year, it would be nearly empty. It would not attract. The public would not enter it. The bookseller would expire, and his family would go on the dole."

"Critics have been known to contract mortal 'occupational diseases' of the mind from a steady diet of bad books."

"The test of a first-rate work, and, a test of your sincerity in calling it a first-rate work, is that you finish it."

"It is impossible to read properly without using all one's engine-power. If we are not tired after reading, common-sense is not in us."

"Essential characteristic of the really great novelist: a Christ-like, all-embracing compassion."

JESSE LEE BENNETT
1885–1931

"Books are the compasses and telescopes and sextants and charts which other men have prepared to help us navigate the dangerous seas of human life."

RICHARD BENTLEY
1662–1742

"I hold it as certain, that no man was ever written out of reputation but by himself."

WILLIAM BERKELEY
1601–1677

"I thank God that we have no free schools nor printing. And I hope we shall not have these in three hundred years. For learning has brought disobedience and heresy and sects into the world, and printing has divulged them and libels against the government."

MARY MCLEOD BETHUNE
1875–1955

"The whole world opened to me when I learned to read."

JOHN BETJEMAN
1906–1984

"One of the silliest questions you can ask a book collector is, 'Have you read all these?' Of course he hasn't. Some books are bought to look at, not to read."

THE BIBLE

"Of making many books there is no end; and much study is a weariness of the flesh." (Ecclesiastes)

"Now go, write it before them in a table, and note it in a book." (Isaiah)

"Even the world itself could not contain the books that should be written." (John)

"Oh that my words were now written! Oh that they were printed in a book!" (Job)

"My desire is . . . that mine adversary had written a book." (Job)

"What thou seest, write in a book. . . ." (Revelation)

"Who is worthy to open the book, and to loose the seals thereof?" (Revelation)

"Another book was opened, which is the book of life." (Revelation)

AMBROSE BIERCE
1842–1914

"Every book that is worth reading is founded on something permanent in human nature or the constitution of things, and constructed with principles of art which are themselves eternal. Whether it is read in one decade or another—even in one century or another—is of no importance; its value and charm are unchanged and unchangeable."

"Circumlocution, *n.* A literary trick whereby the writer who has nothing to say breaks it gently to the reader."

"History, *n.* An account mostly false, of events mostly unimportant, which are brought about by rulers mostly knaves, and soldiers mostly fools."

JOSH BILLINGS
1818–1885

"A learned fool is one who has read everything and remembered it."

JAMES H. BILLINGTON
1929–

"Libraries are starting places for the adventure of learning that can go on whatever one's vocation and location in life. Reading is an adventure like that of discovery itself. Libraries are our base camp."

HORACE BINNEY
1780–1875

"I certainly think that the best book in the world would owe the most to a good Index, and the worst book, if it had but a single good thought in it, might be kept alive by it."

AUGUSTINE BIRRELL
1850–1933

"A great library easily begets affection, which may deepen into love."

"There is no collector, not even the basest of them all, the Belial of his tribe, the man who collects money, whose sense of the joys of ownership is keener than the book-collector."

"All the best books are necessarily second-hand."

"To be proud of having two thousand books would be absurd. You might as well be proud of having two topcoats. After your first two thousand difficulty begins, but until you have ten thousand volumes the less you say about your library the better. *Then* you may begin to speak."

"Reading is not a duty, and has consequently no business to be made disagreeable."

"Good as it is to inherit a library, it is better to collect one."

"Libraries are not made; they grow."

"To listen to some people, you might almost fancy it was within their power to build a barricade of books, and sit behind it mocking the slings and arrows of outrageous fortune."

"Book hunting is a respectable pursuit, an agreeable pastime, an aid to study—but so are many other pastimes and pursuits. Well it would be if historians of book hunting caught but a little of the graceful simplicity and sincerity of an Isaac Walton or a Gilbert White. But no! for the most part these historians are masses of affectation, boasters of bargains, retailers of prices, never touching the heart or refining the fancy. . . . Sham raptures over rare volumes, and bombastic accounts of by-gone auctions, have never helped to swell the ranks of the noble army of book hunters."

"Of all odd crazes, the craze to be forever reading new books is one of the oddest."

WILLIAM BLAKE
1757–1827

"I was in a printing house in Hell, and saw the method in which knowledge is transmitted from generation to generation."

"The reason Milton wrote in fetters when he wrote of Angels and God, and at liberty when of Devils and Hell, is because he was a true Poet, and of the Devil's party without knowing it."

S. LAMAN BLANCHARD
1804–1845

"Behold the bookshelf of a dunce
Who borrows—never lends:
Yon work, in twenty volumes, once
Belonged to twenty friends."

THEODORE C. BLEGEN
1891–1969

"Without disparaging the other forms of collecting, I confess a conviction that the human impulse to collect reaches one of its highest levels in the domain of books."

"[Books] are a major part of the documentation of humanity. Life without them is man devoid of memory. Life with them is a gateway to the understanding of past and present."

"Books are books, but they are also men speaking to present and future—human extensions beyond locality and grave. They are records, documents, sources, heritage, literature, creative ideas given life and clothed with form. They are the recorded sum of human wisdom and folly, learning and ignorance, beauty and ugliness, nobility and sordidness, faith and despair."

MARGUERITE BLESSINGTON
1789–1849

". . . if those only wrote, who were sure of being read, we should have fewer authors; and the shelves of libraries would not groan beneath the weight of dusty tomes more voluminous than luminous."

ANTHONY BLOND
1928–

"Editors have to be able to spell; publishers can be illiterate."

"The romantic novel brigade are a formidable band— mostly women, often wealthy, occasionally heads of Oxford women's colleges."

GIAMBATTISTA BODONI
1740–1813

"The beauty of letters consists in their regularity, in their clearness, and in their conformity to the taste of the race, nation, and age in which the work was first written, and finally in the grace of the characters independent of time or place."

"No other art is more justified than typography in looking ahead to future centuries; for the creations of typography benefit coming generations as much as present ones."

NICOLAS BOILEAU-DESPRÉAUX
1636–1711

"A book displeases you? Who forces you to read it?"

ROBERT BOLT
1924–1995

" 'He [Lord Byron] writes like a housewife on the verge of the vapors.' "

ERMA BOMBECK
1927–

"Reading is an opportunity, a privilege to meet people you've never seen in places you've never been before."

DANIEL J. BOORSTIN
1914–

"A best-seller was a book which somehow sold well simply because it was selling well."

JORGE LUIS BORGES
1899–1986

"To arrange a library is to practice in a quaint and modest way the art of criticism."

"I have always come to life after coming to books."

"I have always imagined that Paradise will be a kind of library."

CHRISTIAN NESTELL BOVEE
1820–1904

"Books only partially represent their authors; the writer is always greater than his work."

"There is probably no hell for authors in the next world—they suffer so much from critics and publishers in this."

CATHERINE DRINKER BOWEN
1879–1973

"Writing, I think, is not apart from living. Writing is a kind of double living. The writer experiences everything twice. Once in reality and once in that mirror which waits always before or behind."

"In writing biography, fact and fiction shouldn't be mixed. And if they are, the fiction parts should be printed in red ink, the fact parts in black ink."

FREDSON BOWERS
1905–1991

"That five hundred may busy themselves in the general collection for the one who reads in the rare-book room means little when quality, not quantity, is the criterion."

RAY BRADBURY
1920–

"Afternoons, when the fossil sea was warm and motionless, and the wine trees stood stiff in the yard, and the little distant Martian bone town was all enclosed, and no one drifted out their doors, you could see Mr. K. himself in his room, reading from a metal book with raised hieroglyphs over which he brushed his hand, as one might play a harp. And from the book, as his fingers stroked, a voice sang, a soft ancient voice, which told tales of when the sea was red steam on the shore and ancient men had carried clouds of metal insects and electronic spiders into battle."

BEN BRADLEE
1921–

"To determine how long it will take to write a book, figure out how long it should take, double it and add six months."

TOM BRADLEY
1917–

"While other students were out playing I would often slip into my seat during recess and read a book."

JOHANNES BRAHMS
1833–1897

"I always write only half-sentences, and the reader himself must supply the other half."

JOHN BRAINE
1922–1986

"Being a writer in a library is rather like being a eunuch in a harem."

DOROTHEA BRANDE
1893–1948

"Fiction supplies the only philosophy that many readers know; it establishes their ethical, social, and material standards; it confirms them in their prejudices or opens their minds to a wider world."

SEBASTIAN BRANDT
1458–1521

"The Book-Fool is the man, not who wasted good money on worthless books, but who could not, or would not, read the good books he bought."

RICHARD BRAUTIGAN
1935–1984

"I wonder whether what we are publishing now is worth cutting down trees to make paper for the stuff."

KATE BRAVERMAN
1950–

"In Communist countries, you execute your poets. In the free world, the poets execute themselves."

CHARLES BRAY
1811–1884

"Books to me, that is, those of our best writers, are ever new; the books may be the same, but I am changed. Every seven years gives me a different, often a higher, appreciation of those I like. Every good book is worth reading three times at least."

BERTOLT BRECHT
1898–1956

"Literature has the right and the duty to give to the public the ideas of the time."

STUART BRENT
1915–

"I had decided to become a bookseller because I loved good books. I assumed there must be many others who shared a love for reading and that I could minister to their needs. I thought of this as a calling. It never occurred to me to investigate bookselling as a business."

"It hurt me terribly if someone came in and asked for a book without letting me talk with him about it. The whole joy of selling a book was in talking about the ideas in it. It was a matter of sharing my life and my thought and my very blood stream with others."

"When I began to read, I fell in love with such consuming passion that I became a threat to everyone who knew me. Whatever I was reading, I became: I was the character, Hamlet or Lear; I was the author Shelley or Stendahl. When I was seized by sudden quirks, jerks, and strange gestures, it was not because I was a nervous child—I was being some character."

NICHOLAS BRETON
1545?–1626

"And tell prose writers, stories are so stale,
That penny ballads have a better sale."

REGINALD A. BREWER
1899–1985

"For generations the bibliophile has been pictured in the public mind as a dry-as-dust scholar or a veritable Croesus. It has been the gradual breaking down of this fallacious conception—the realization that it is not necessary to profess a love of old, musty tomes nor even to be richly endowed—that has opened up the pleasures of book collecting for thousands of book lovers. For every man of deep learning finding enjoyment in surrounding himself with volumes of a bygone age, hundreds of modern-minded collectors are finding equal pleasures in books as young as themselves. . . . All the thrill and excitement of the chase are open to the man of meagre purse, and one can qualify as a genuine bibliomaniac without ever stepping out of the twentieth century."

JOHN BRIGHT
1811–1889

"Books, it is true, are silent as you see them on their shelves; but, silent as they are, when I enter a library I feel as if almost the dead were present, and I know if I put questions to these books they will answer me with all the faithfulness and fulness which has been left in them by the great men who have left the books with us."

CHARLOTTE BRONTË
1816–1855

"When authors write best, or, at least, when they write most fluently, an influence seems to waken in them, which becomes their master—which will have its own way—putting out of view all behests but its own, dictating certain words, and insisting on their being used, whether vehement or measured in their nature; new-moulding characters, giving unthought-of turns to incidents, rejecting carefully-elaborated old ideas, and suddenly creating and adopting new ones."

"Novelists should never allow themselves to weary of the study of real life."

"Thackeray likes to dissect an ulcer or an aneurism; he has pleasure in putting his cruel knife or probe into quivering, living flesh. Thackeray would not like all the world to be good."

"I wish critics would judge me as an *author*, not as a woman."

GWENDOLYN BROOKS
1917–

"Reading is important—read between the lines. Don't swallow everything."

"I am a writer perhaps *because* I am not a talker."

VAN WYCK BROOKS
1886–1963

"No man should ever publish a book until he has first read it to a woman."

ALICE WILLIAMS BROTHERTON
D. 1930

"Books we must have though we lack bread."

HENRY BROUGHAM
1778–1868

"It is well to read everything of something, and something of everything."

HEYWOOOD BROUN
1888–1939

"The great threat to the young and pure in heart is not what they read, but what they don't read."

RITA MAE BROWN
1944–

"Don't ask to live in tranquil times. Literature doesn't grow there."

"Money and writing appear to be mutually exclusive."

"I believe all literature started as gossip."

"It's an act of faith to be a writer in a postliterate world."

WILLIAM H. BROWN
1765–1793

"To dip into any book burthens the mind with unnecessary lumber, and may rather be called a disadvantage than a benefit."

"Among all kinds of knowledge which arise from reading, self-knowledge is eminent."

WILLIAM BROWNE
1692–1774

"The King to Oxford sent a troop of horse,
For Tories own no argument but force:
With equal skill to Cambridge books he sent,
For Whigs admit no force but argument."

ELIZABETH BARRETT BROWNING
1806–1861

"Books, books, books:
I have found the secret of a garret room
Piled high with cases in my father's name,
Piled high, packed large,—where, creeping in and out
Among the giant fossils of my past,
Like some small nimble mouse between the ribs
Of a mastadon, I nibbled here and there
At this or that box, pulling through the gap,
In heats of terror, haste, victorious joy,
The first book first. And how I felt it beat
Under my pillow, in the morning's dark,
An hour before the sun would let me read!
My books! At last because the time was ripe,
I chanced upon the poets."

"I have *worked* at poetry—it has not been to me reverie, but art. As the physician and lawyer work at their several professions, so have I, and so do I, apply to mine."

"I read books bad and good—some bad and good
At once (good aims not always make good books.)"

"We all generally err by reading too much, and out of proportion to what we think. I should be wiser, I am persuaded, if I had not read half as much—should have had stronger and better faculties. The fact is, that the *ne plus ultra* of intellectual indolence is this reading of books. It comes next to what the Americans call 'whittling.' "

"Many a fervid man
Writes books as cold and flat as graveyard stones."

"Books succeed,
And lives fail."

ROBERT BROWNING
1812–1889

"Plague take all your pedants, say I!
He who wrote what I hold in my hand,
Centuries back was so good as to die,
Leaving this rubbish to cumber the land."

"You, for example, clever to a fault,
The rough and ready man who write apace,
Read somewhat less, think perhaps even less."

GUSTAVE BRUNET
1807–1896

"The choice of books, like the toilet of gentility, is governed by fashion, whose laws admit of no appeal."

JAMES BRYCE
1838–1922

"Life is too short for reading inferior books."

EGERTON BRYDGES
1762–1837

"Of all the human relaxations which are free from guilt, none so dignified as reading."

JOHN SHEFFIELD, FIRST DUKE OF BUCKINGHAM AND NORMANBY
1648–1721

"Learn to write well, or not to write at all."

JOHN BUNYAN
1628–1688

"Go now, my little Book, to every place
Where my first Pilgrim has but shown his face."

ANTHONY BURGESS
1917–1993

"The possession of a book becomes a substitute for reading it."

"There is usually something wrong with writers the young like."

"To read without reflecting, is like eating without digesting."

FANNY BURNEY
1752–1840

"A lady should never degrade herself by being put on a level with writers, and such sort of people."

"The assailants of the quill have their honor as much at heart as the assailants of the sword."

"To avoid what is common, without adopting what is unnatural, must limit the ambition of the vulgar herd of authors."

ERIC BURNS
1950–

"Give a man a hoe and he is something to exploit. Give him a book and he is something to fear."

ROBERT BURNS
1759–1796

"Through and through th' inspired leaves,
Ye maggots, make your windings;

But O, respect his lordship's taste,
And spare his golden bindings!"

"Some books are lies frae end to end."

JOHN BURROUGHS
1837–1921

"How much there is in books that one does not want to know, that it would be a mere weariness and burden to the spirit to know."

"I go to books and to nature as a bee goes to the flower, for a nectar that I can make into my own honey."

WILLIAM S. BURROUGHS
1914–

"Writing's an important way of living."

ABE BURROWS & JO SWERLING
1910–1985 1897–

" 'I want a normal life, with wallpaper and bookends.' "

JOHN HILL BURTON
1809–1881

"It is difficult, almost impossible, to find a book in which something either valuable or amusing may not be found, if the proper alembic be applied."

"Books are not good fuel. . . . In the days when heretical books were burned, it was necessary to place them on large wooden stages, and after all the pains were taken to demolish them, considerable readable masses were sometimes found in the embers; whence it was supposed that the devil, conversant in fire and its effects, gave them his special protection. In the end it was found easier and cheaper to burn the heretics themselves than their books."

ROBERT BURTON
1577–1640

"I no sooner come into the library, but I bolt the door, excluding lust, ambition, avarice . . . in the lap of eternity amongst so many divine souls, I take my seat with so lofty a spirit and sweet content that I pity all our great ones and rich men who know not this happiness."

"To most kind of men it is an extraordinary delight to study, for what a world of books offers itself, in all subjects, arts, and sciences, to the sweet content and capacity of the Reader!"

"They lard their lean books with the fat of others' works."

RICHARD DE BURY
1287–1345

"A library of wisdom, is more precious than all wealth, and all things that are desirable cannot be compared to it. Whoever therefore claims to be zealous of truth, of happiness, of wisdom or knowledge, aye even of the faith, must needs become a lover of books."

"What delightful teaching there is in books. How easily, how secretly, how safely in books do we make bare without shame the poverty of human ignorance! These are the masters that instruct us without rod and ferrule, without words of anger, without payment of money or clothing. Should ye approach them, they are not asleep; if ye seek to answer them, they do not hide themselves; should ye err, they do not chide; and should ye show ignorance, they know not how to laugh."

"In books I find the dead as if they were alive; in books I foresee things to come; in books warlike affairs are set forth; from books come forth the laws of peace. All things are corrupted and decay in time; . . . all the glory of the world would be buried in oblivion, unless God had provided mortals with the remedy of books."

"Books delight us, when prosperity smiles upon us; they comfort us inseparably when stormy fortune frowns on us. They lend validity to human compacts, and no serious judgments are propounded without their help. Arts and sciences, all the advantages of which no mind can enumerate, consist in books. How highly must we estimate the wondrous power of books, since through them we survey the utmost bounds of the world and time, and contemplate the things that are as well as those that are not, as in the mirror of eternity."

SAMUEL BUTLER
1835–1902

"Books want to be born: I never make them. They come to me and insist on being written, and on being such and such."

"Editors are like the people who bought and sold in the book of Revelation; there is not one but has the mark of the beast upon him."

"Writing for reviews or newspapers is bad training for one who may aspire to write works of more permanent interest."

"Some poets always begin to get groggy about the knees after running for seven or eight lines."

"An Apology for the Devil: It must be remembered that we have only heard one side of the case. God has written all the books."

"Affects all books of past and modern ages,
But reads no further than their title-pages."

"The oldest books are still only just out to those who have not read them."

"*The Ancient Mariner* would not have been taken so well if it had been called *The Old Sailor*."

GEORGE GORDON NOEL BYRON
1788–1824

" 'Tis pleasant, sure, to see one's name in print;
A book's a book, although there's nothing in 't."

"I read eating, read in bed; read when no one else reads."

"For a man to become a poet . . . he must be in love, or miserable."

"Gin-and-water is the source of all my inspiration."

"I never wrote anything worth mentioning till I was in love."

ANNA RAY CHATMAN
HER BOOK

ERSKINE CALDWELL
1903–1987

"I think you must remember that a writer is a simple-minded person to begin with and go on that basis. He's not a great mind, he's not a great thinker, he's not a great philosopher, he's a story-teller."

CALLIMACHUS
THIRD CENTURY B.C.

"A big book is a big nuisance."

THOMAS CAMPBELL
1777–1844

"Gentlemen, I agree with you that Napoleon is a tyrant, a monster, the sworn foe of our nation. But, gentlemen—he once shot a publisher."

"Now Barabbas was a publisher."

ALBERT CAMUS
1913–1960

"What, in fact, is a novel but a universe in which action is endowed with form, where final words are pronounced, where people possess one another completely, and where life assumes the aspect of destiny?"

TRUMAN CAPOTE
1924–1984

"Late one afternoon, while waiting for a Fifth Avenue bus, I noticed a taxi stop across the street to let out a girl who ran up the steps of the Forty-Second Street public library. She was through the doors before I recognized her, which was pardonable, for Holly and libraries were not an easy association to make."

"Finishing a book is just like you took a child out in the yard and shot it."

THOMAS CARLYLE
1795–1881

"After all manner of professors have done their best for us, the place we are to get knowledge is in books. The true university of these days is a collection of books."

"In books lies the *soul* of the whole Past Time; the articulate audible voice of the Past, when the body and material substance of it has altogether vanished like a dream."

"All that Mankind has done, thought, gained, or been is lying as in magic preservation in the pages of Books."

"There is nothing more injurious to the faculties than to keep poring over books continually without attempting to exhibit any of our own conceptions."

"He who first shortened the labour of copyists by device of *Movable Types* was disbanding hired armies, and cashiering most Kings and Senates, and creating a whole new democratic world: he had invented the art of printing."

"If a book comes from the heart, it will contrive to reach other hearts."

"Books are a triviality. Life alone is great."

"Of all priesthoods, aristocracies, governing classes at present extant in the world, there is no class comparable for importance to that priesthood of the writers of books."

"A well-written life is almost as rare as a well-spent one."

"What a sad want I am in of libraries, of books to gather facts from! Why is there not a Majesty's library in every country town? There is a Majesty's gaol and gallows in every one."

"Readers are not aware of the fact, but a fact it is of daily increasing magnitude, and already of terrible importance to readers, that their first grand necessity in reading is to be vigilantly, conscientiously *select*; and to know everywhere that books, like human souls, are actually divided into what we may call 'sheep and goats.' "

"A library is not worth anything without a catalogue—it is a Polyphemus without any eye in his head."

"Are we not drive to the conclusion that of the things which man can do or make here below, by far the most momentous, wonderful, and worthy are the things called Books?"

LEWIS CARROLL
1832–1898

" 'And what is the use of a book,' thought Alice, 'without pictures or conversation?' "

JOHN CARTER
1905–1975

"Book-collecting is at once the most various, the most sophisticated, and the least income-taxing of the major forms of connoisseurship."

"In some bibliophily is induced by circumstances, for others it is contagious, in others again it is a natural by-product or development from the process of forming a library. No one, I think, would contend that book-collectors are born rather than made. Hereditary bibliophily is of the rarest occurrence in history, and the exceptions are so pitifully few that even Mendel would have labelled them as sports rather than as instances of the inheritance of acquired characteristics."

BARBARA CARTLAND
1901–

"I never read any novels except my own. When I feel worried, agitated or upset, I read one and find the last pages soothe me and leave me happy. I quite understand why I am popular in hospitals."

JOYCE CARY
1888–1957

"It is very pleasant to be written up, even by a writer."

GIACAMO CASANOVA
1725–1798

"Two or three weeks after my arrival, the Prince of Santa Croce heard me complaining of the obstacles to research in Roman libraries, and he offered to give me an introduction to the Superior of the Jesuits. I accepted the offer, and was made free of the library; I could not only go and read when I liked, but I could, on writing my name down, take books away with me. The keepers of the library always brought me candles when it grew dark, and their politeness was so great that they gave me the key of a side door, so that I could slip in and out as I pleased."

VERA CASPARY
1904–1987

"When, during the 1936 campaign, I learned that the President was a devotee of mystery stories, I voted a straight Republican ticket."

WILLA CATHER
1873–1947

"Most of the basic material a writer works with is acquired before the age of fifteen."

"There are only two or three human stories, and they go on repeating themselves as fiercely as if they had never happened before."

MIGUEL DE CERVANTES SAAVEDRA
1547–1616

"There's no book so bad that something good may not be found in it."

" 'Woe is me! I am verily persuaded, and it is as certainly true as I was born to die, that these cursed books of knight-errantry which he keeps, and is so often reading, have turned his brain; and now I think of it, I have often heard him say, talking to himself, that he would turn knight-errant, and go about the world in quest of adventures. The devil and Barabbas take all such books, that have thus spoiled the finest understanding in all La Mancha.' "

"Whilst Don Quixote still slept on, the priest asked the niece for the keys of the chamber where the books were, those authors of the mischief.... They found above a hundred volumes in folio, very well bound, besides a great many small ones. And no sooner did the housekeeper see them, than she ran out of the room in great haste, and immediately returned with a pot of holy water and a bunch of hyssop, and said: Senor Licentiate, take this and sprinkle the room, lest some enchanter, of the many these books abound with should enchant us in revenge for what we intend to do, in banishing them out of the world."

"There are some who write and fling books broadcast on the world as if they were fritters."

SEBASTIAN-ROCH-NICOLAS CHAMFORT
1741–1794

"Most contemporary books give the impression of having been manufactured in a day, out of books read the day before."

"What is responsible for the success of many works is the rapport between the mediocrity of the author's ideas and the mediocrity of the public's."

RAYMOND CHANDLER
1888–1959

"The thriller is an extension of the fairy tale. It is melodrama so embellished as to create the illusion that the story being told, however unlikely, could be true."

" 'So you're a story writer too, huh? The detective business must be on the skids—what are you trying to do—elevate yourself?' "

" 'I'd decided I'd write about a murder; it's safer. Besides, they tell me the profits are good.' "

"When the plot flags, bring in a man with a gun."

"When I split an infinitive, god damn it, I split it so it stays split."

WILLIAM ELLERY CHANNING
1780–1842

"Every man is a volume if you know how to read him."

"The best books for man are not always those which the wise recommend, but often those which meet the peculiar wants, the natural thirst of his mind, and therefore awaken interest and rival thought."

"It is chiefly through books that we enjoy the intercourse with superior minds. . . . In the best books, great men talk to us, give us their most precious thoughts, and pour their souls into ours. God be thanked for books."

"Let every man, if possible, gather some good books under his roof, and obtain access for himself and family to some social library. Almost any luxury should be sacrificed to this."

"Books are the true levellers. They give to all, who will faithfully use them, the society, the spiritual presence, of the best and greatest of our race."

GEORGE CHAPMAN
1559?–1634?

"And let a scholar all Earth's volumes carry,
He will be but a walking dictionary."

MELVIN CHAPMAN
1928–

"Reading people are ruling people."

ELIZABETH RUNDLE CHARLES
1828–1896

"But the way to wealth through the quill seems long."

ILKA CHASE
1905–1978

"I suppose anyone who has ever written a travel book has had the experience of being accosted by a reader with blood in his eye and a lawsuit in his voice."

FRANCOIS-RENÉ DE CHATEAUBRIAND
1768–1848

"The original writer is not he who refrains from imitating others, but he who can be imitated by none."

GEOFFREY CHAUCER
1340?–1400

"And as for me, thogh that I can but lyte,
On bokes for to rede I me delyte,
And to hem yeve I feyth and ful credence,
And in myn herte have hem in reverence
So hertely, that ther is game noon,
That fro my bokes maketh me to goon."

"For him was lever have at his bedded heed
Twenty bokes, clad in blak or reed,
Of Aristotle and his philosophye,
Than robes riche, or fithele, or gay sautrye."

"For out of old feldes, as men seith,
Cometh al this newe corn fro yere to yere;
And out of olde bokes, in good feith,
Cometh al this newe science that men lere."

"So when I saw I might not slepe,
Til now late, this other night,
Upon my bedde I sat upright,
And bad oon reche me a boke,
A romaunce, and he hit me took
To rede and dryve the night away."

GEORGE B. CHEEVER
1807–1890

"A man who writes an immoral but immortal book may be tracked into eternity by a procession of lost souls from every generation, every one to be witness against him at the judgment, to show to him and to the universe the immeasurableness of his iniquity."

JOHN CHEEVER
1912–1982

"My definition of a good editor is a man I think charming, who sends me large checks, praises my work, my physical beauty, my sexual prowess, and who has a stranglehold on the publisher and the bank."

"Plot implies narrative and a lot of crap."

"Good writers are more often excellent at a hundred other things, but writing promises a greater latitude for the ego."

"Any memory of pain is deeply buried, and there is nothing more painful for a writer than an inability to work."

ANTON CHEKHOV
1860–1904

"In literature the lower ranks are as necessary as in the army."

"How pleasant it is to respect people! When I see books, I am not concerned with how the authors loved or played cards; I see only their marvelous works."

"Critics are like horseflies which prevent the horse from plowing."

LORD CHESTERFIELD
1694–1773

"Due attention to the inside of books, and due contempt for the outside, is the proper relation between a man of sense and his books."

"Wear your learning like your watch, in a private pocket; and do not pull it out, and strike it, merely to show that you have one."

"Let blockheads read what blockheads wrote."

G. K. CHESTERTON
1874–1936

"A good novel tells us the truth about its hero; but a bad novel tells us the truth about its author."

"The book originated in the suggestion of a publisher; as many more good books have done than the arrogance of the man of letters is commonly inclined to admit."

"The Iliad is only great because all life is a battle, the Odyssey because all life is a journey, the Book of Job because all life is a riddle."

"There is a great deal of difference between the eager man who wants to read a book, and the tired man who wants a book to read."

"The human race, to which so many of my readers belong. . . ."

"Mr. [G. B.] Shaw is (I suspect) the only man on earth who has never written any poetry."

"Literature is a luxury; fiction is a necessity."

CHARLES W. CHESTNUTT
1858–1932

"I think I must write a book. I am almost afraid to undertake a book so early and with so little experience in composition. But it has been my cherished dream . . . knowledge of the classics, acquaintance with the modern languages, an intimate friendship with literature, etc., seven years in the schoolroom, two years of married life, and a habit of studying character have not left me unprepared to write even a book."

BEVERLY CHEW
1850–1924

"Old Books are best! With what delight
Does 'Faithorne fecit' greet our sight."

HAROLD H. CHILD
1869–1945

"It would seem as if there had been a conspiracy to make a bookish thing of me, when I was meant to be a gardener, a hunting man, a soldier, a whiskey-taster, or something wholesome like that."

LYDIA M. CHILD
1802–1880

"I was gravely warned by some of my female acquaintances that no woman could expect to be regarded as a lady after she had written a book."

RUFUS CHOATE
1799–1859

"A book is the only immortality."

AGATHA CHRISTIE
1891–1975

"I've always believed in writing without a collaborator, because where two people are writing the same book, each believes he gets all the worry and only half the royalties."

"The best time for planning a book is while you're doing the dishes."

CHARLES CHURCHILL
1731–1764

"Sleep over books and leave mankind unknown."

"Though by whim, envy, or resentment led,
They damn those authors whom they never read."

"With various readings stored his empty skull,
Learn'd without sense, and venerably dull."

WINSTON CHURCHILL
1874–1965

"It is a good thing for an uneducated man to read books of quotations."

"Writing is an adventure. To begin with, it is a toy and an amusement. Then it becomes a mistress, then it becomes a master, then it becomes a tyrant. The last phase is that just as you are about to be reconciled to your servitude, you kill the monster and fling him to the public."

"If you cannot read all your books, at any rate handle, or as it were, fondle them—peer into them, let them fall open where they will, read from the first sentence that arrests the eye, set them back on the shelves with your own hands, arrange them on your own plan so that you at least know where they are. Let them be your friends; let them at any rate be your acquaintances."

MARCUS TULLIUS CICERO
106–43 B.C.

"A room without books is a body without a soul."

"[Books] nourish youth; delight old age; adorn prosperity; afford a refuge and solace in adversity; forming our delights at home; anything but hindrances abroad; they are our nightly associates; our indoor and out-of-door companions."

"I can study my books at any time, for they are always disengaged."

"Let us assume that entertainment is the sole end of reading; even so, I think you would hold that no mental employment is so broadening to the sympathies or so enlightening to the understanding. Other pursuits belong not to all times, all ages, all conditions; but this gives stimulus to our youth and diversion to our old age; this adds a charm to our success, and offers a haven of consolation to failure. Through the night-watches, on all our journeyings, and in our hours of ease, it is our unfailing companion."

EMILE CIORAN
1911–1995

"Everybody is writing books and I am beginning to find it disgusting."

JOHN CLARE
1793–1864

"It is common in villages to pass judgment on a lover of books as a sure indication of laziness."

SAMUEL L. CLEMENS
1835–1910

"You ask me where I spend my evenings. Where do you suppose, with a free prentice library containing more than four thousand volumes within a quarter of a mile of me and nobody at home to talk to."

"I like a thin book because it will steady a table, a leather volume because it will strop a razor, and a heavy book because it can be thrown at a cat."

"A very good library could be started by leaving Jane Austen out."

"In one place in *The Deerslayer*, and in the restricted space of two-thirds of a page, Cooper has scored 114 offences against literary art out of a possible 115. It breaks the record."

"There are three infallible ways of pleasing an author, and the three form a rising scale of compliment: 1, to tell him you have read one of his books; 2, to tell him you have read all of his books; 3, to ask him to let you read the manuscript of his forthcoming book. No. 1 admits you to his respect; No. 2 admits you to his admiration; No. 3 carries you clear into his heart."

"A classic is something that everybody wants to have and nobody wants to read."

"She warn't particular, she could write about anything you choose to give her to write about, just so it was sadful."

"There ain't nothing more to write about and I'm rotten glad of it, because if I'd a knowd what a trouble it was to make a book, I wouldn't a tackled it, and ain't a-going to no more."

"Take an idiot man from a lunatic asylum and marry him to an idiot woman, and the fourth generation of this connection should be a good publisher from the American point of view."

"The very ink with which all history is written is merely fluid prejudice."

"Biographers are but the clothes and buttons of the man—the biography of the man himself cannot be written."

"The difference between the almost-right word and the right word is really a large matter—it's the difference between the lightning-bug and the lightning."

"Persons attempting to find a motive in this narrative will be prosecuted; persons attempting to find a moral in it will be banished; persons attempting to find a plot in it will be shot."

"As to the adjective: when in doubt, strike it out."

"Whenever the literary German dives into a sentence, that is the last you are going to see of him till he emerges on the other side of his Atlantic with his verb in his mouth."

WILLIAM L. CLEMENTS
1861–1934

"If a man is even moderately enthusiastic, and has actually collected a sufficient number of books to make a foundation of a library as a specific subject, he, by general understanding among his co-sufferers, has been inoculated with the disease and has a case of Bibliomania, the severity of which increases or decreases in direct proportion to the patient's enthusiasm and self-sacrifice to attain the end he has in view. Friends of the patient look upon him possibly with sympathy, but always with an eye of pity, and members of his family speak of his trouble with indignation and sometimes shame, if his excesses in purchasing rare books, even though entirely within his subject, encroach in any way upon the normal activities of the family and upon the expenses connected therewith."

ARTHUR HUGH CLOUGH
1819–1861

"A bad style is as bad as bad manners."

IRVIN S. COBB
1876–1944

"I couldn't write the things they publish now, with no beginning and no end, and a little incest in the middle."

THOMAS J. COBDEN-SANDERSON
1840–1922

"Some subtle relationship there may be, and should be, between the inside and the outside of a book, between its contents and ornamentation."

"When I print a book or bind one it is because I have a message in my soul which I am impelled to give to mankind, and it comes out through my fingers. Other men express their messages in different *media,*—in stone or on canvas. I have discovered that the book is my medium."

ALEXANDER COCKBURN
1802–1880

"Happy is he who, when the day's work is done, finds his rest, and solace, and recreation in communion with the master minds of the present and the past—in study, in literature, and the enjoyment of pleasures which are to be derived from this source."

JEAN COCTEAU
1889–1963

"The greatest masterpiece in literature is only a dictionary out of order."

"What is history after all? History is facts which become lies in the end; legends and lies which become history in the end."

"Listen carefully to first criticisms of your work. Note just what it is about your work that the critics don't like—then cultivate it. That's the part of your work that's individual and worth keeping."

"What is style? For many people, a very complicated way of saying very simple things. According to us, a very simple way of saying very complicated things."

BARBARA K. COHEN
1932–1993

"I went to the library. They gave you books for nothing. You had to bring them back, but when you did, they let you take others."

HARTLEY COLERIDGE
1796–1849

"There is no such thing as a worthless book, though there are some far worse than worthless; no book which is not worth preserving, if its existence may be tolerated; as there are some men whom it may be proper to hang, but none who should be suffered to starve."

SAMUEL T. COLERIDGE
1772–1834

"Readers may be divided into four classes: 1. Sponges, who absorb all they read and return it nearly in the same state, only a little dirtied. 2. Sand-glasses, who retain nothing and are content to get through a book for the sake of getting through the time. 3. Strain-bags, who retain merely the dregs of what they read. 4. Mogul diamonds, equally rare and valuable, who profit by what they read, and enable others to profit by it also."

"I could inform the dullest author how he might write an interesting book. Let him relate the events of his own life with honesty, not disguising the feelings that accompanied them."

"Gibbon's style is detestable, but his style is not the worst thing about him. His history has proved an effective bar to all real familiarity with the temper and habits of imperial Rome."

"Prose = words in their best order;—poetry = the *best* words in the best order."

"Until you understand a writer's ignorance, presume yourself ignorant of his understanding."

"It is saying less than the truth to affirm that an excellent book (and the remark holds almost equally good of a Raphael as of a Milton) is like a well-chosen and well-tended fruit tree. Its fruits are not of one season only. With the due and natural intervals, we may recur to it year after year, and it will supply the same nourishment and the same gratification, if only we ourselves return to it with the same healthful appetite."

COLETTE
1873–1954

"Sit down and put down everything that comes into your head and then you're a writer. But an author is one who can judge his own stuff's worth, without pity, and destroy most of it."

"When one can read, can penetrate the enchanting world of books, why write?"

"The writer who loses his self-doubt, who gives way as he grows old to a sudden euphoria, to prolixity, should stop writing immediately: the time has come for him to lay aside his pen."

JEREMY COLLIER
1650–1726

"Books are a guide in youth, and an entertainment for age. They support us under solitude, and keep us from becoming a burden to ourselves. They help us to forget the crossness of men and things, compose our cares and our passions, and lay our disappointments asleep. When we are weary of the living, we may repair to the dead, who have nothing of peevishness, pride, or design in their conversation."

"A man may as well expect to grow stronger by always eating, as wiser by always Reading. Too much overcharges Nature, and turns more into Disease than Nourishment. 'Tis Thought and Digestion which makes Books serviceable, and gives Health and Vigour to the Mind."

MARVA COLLINS
1936–

"Readers are leaders. Thinkers succeed."

WILKIE COLLINS
1824–1889

"I wonder whether the gentlemen who make a business and living out of writing books ever find their own selves getting in the way of their subjects like me?"

"Haven't I seen you the reader with the greatest authors in your hands, and don't I know how ready your attention is to wander when it's a book that asks for it, instead of a person?"

"It may be possible in novel-writing to present characters successfully without telling a story; but it is not possible to tell a story successfully without presenting characters."

ARTHUR W. COLTON
1868–1943

"It is poor traveling that is only to arrive, and it is poor reading that is only to find out how the book ends."

CHARLES C. COLTON
1780–1832

"Next to acquiring good friends, the best acquisition is that of good books."

"If we steal thoughts from the moderns, it will be cried down as plagiarism; if from the ancients, it will be cried up as erudition."

"Many books require no thought from those who read them, and for a very simple reason;—they made no such demand upon those who wrote them."

"That writer does the most, who gives his reader the *most* knowledge, and takes from him the *least* time."

IVY COMPTON-BURNETT
1884–1969

"As regards plots I find real life no help at all. Real life seems to have no plots."

"No writer goes the whole length with any other. Each of them shivers at the lapses of the rest, and is blind to his own.

And the youngest shiver the most. And the greatest writers have them."

CONFUCIUS
551–479 B.C.

"A blemish may be taken out of a diamond by careful polishing; but if your words have the least blemish, there is no way to efface it."

LESLEY CONGER
1922–

"The best of my education has come from the public library . . . my tuition fee is a bus fare and once in a while, five cents a day for an overdue book. You don't need to know very much to start with, if you know the way to the public library."

WILLIAM CONGREVE
1670–1729

"Read, read, sirrah, and refine your appetite; learn to live upon instruction; feast your mind, and mortify your flesh; read, and take your nourishment in at your eyes, shut up your mouth, and chew the cud of understanding."

CYRIL CONNOLLY
1903–1974

"A great writer creates a world of his own, and readers are proud to live in it. A lesser writer may entice them in for a moment, but soon he will watch them filing out."

"I should like to see the custom introduced of readers who are pleased with a book sending the author some small cash token: anything between half-a-crown and a hundred pounds. . . . Not more than a hundred pounds—that would be bad for my character—not less than half-a-crown—that would do no good to yours."

"As repressed sadists are said to become policemen or butchers so those with an irrational fear of life become publishers."

JOSEPH CONRAD
1857–1924

"Of all the inanimate objects, of all men's creations, books are the nearest to us, for they contain our very thoughts, our ambitions, our indignations, our illusions, our fidelity to truth, and our persistent leaning towards error. But most of all they resemble us in their precarious hold on life."

"A word carries far—very far—deals destruction through time as the bullets go flying through space."

"Liberty of the imagination should be the most precious possession of a novelist."

"What is a novel if not a conviction of our fellow-men's existence strong enough to take upon itself a form of imagined life clearer than reality and whose versimilitude of selected episodes puts to shame the pride of documentary history?"

J. GORDON COOGLER
1865–1901

"Alas! for the South, her books have grown fewer—
She never was much given to literature."

ELLIOT COUES
1842–1899

"Bibliography is a necessary nuisance, and a horrible drudgery that no mere drudge could perform. It takes a sort of inspired idiot to be a good bibliographer, and his inspiration is as dangerous a gift as the appetite of the gambler or dipsomaniac—it grows with what it feeds upon, and finally possesses its victim like any other invincible vice. . . . Among the requisite qualifications may be reckoned more zeal than discretion, youth, health, strength, staying powers, unlimited time at command, and access to the [sources]."

NORMAN COUSINS
1912–

"A library is the delivery room for the birth of ideas, a place where history comes to life."

NOEL COWARD
1899–1973

"With my usual watchful eye on posterity, I can only suggest to any wretched future biographer that he gets my daily engagement book and from that fills in anything he can find and good luck to him, poor bugger."

"Madame Bovary is the sexiest book imaginable. The woman's virtually a nymphomaniac but you won't find a vulgar word in the entire thing."

ABRAHAM COWLEY
1618–1667

"Build yourself a book-nest to forget the world without."

"Come my best friends, my books, and lead me on."

"It is a hard and nice thing for a man to write of himself. It grates his own heart to say anything of disparagement, and the reader's ears to hear anything of praise from him."

MALCOLM COWLEY
1898–1989

"No complete son of a bitch ever wrote a good sentence."

WILLIAM COWPER
1731–1800

"Authors hear at length, one general cry,
Tickle and entertain us, or we die!"

"Books are not seldom talismans and spells."

"And has thou sworn, on every slight pretence,
Till perjuries are common as bad pence,
While thousands, careless of the damning sin,
Kiss the book's outside who ne'er look within."

GEORGE CRABBE
1754–1832

"Books cannot always please, however good.
Minds are not ever craving for their food."

"His delight
Was all in books; to read them or to write:
Women and men he strove alike to shun,
And hurried homeward when his tasks were done."

"Who often reads, will sometimes wish to write."

FRANK CRANE
1861–1928

"Let me live and die among books, and when I die let my transmigration be next into a little worm that feeds upon an Elzevir."

STEPHEN CRANE
1871–1900

"Preaching is fatal to art in literature."

ADELAIDE CRAPSEY
1878–1914

"Wouldst thou find my ashes? Look
In the pages of my book;
And, as these thy hands doth turn,
Know here is my funeral urn."

RICHARD CRASHAW
1612?–1649

"Lo here a little volume, but large book."

HECTOR ST. JOHN DE CRÈVECOEUR
1753–1813

"Books tell me so much that they inform me of nothing."

WALTER CRONKITE
1916–

"Whatever the costs of our libraries, the price is cheap compared to that of an ignorant nation."

LAUNCELOT CROSS
1834–1894

"Can any couch be more delectable than the Elysian leaves of books."

BROOKE CRUTCHLEY
1907–

"A well-turned-out book has a serenity which hides every vestige of the disarray which has so often marked its gestation."

BARTON W. CURRIE
1878–1962

"In the tight little cosmos of the fisher of books just one form of collecting is wholly admirable and understandable; namely, the acquisition of rare books and manuscripts. The book collector has known many stamp and coin collectors, old furniture men, old glass and old pewter men who turned to books, but he has never known a first-grade bookman who got down off his hobby before the undertaker was sent for."

"One book at a time, or a very few at a time—there's the ideal way! Bargain a bit, grouse a bit; go home and consult the oracles of bibliography and the auction records; then go back with the gleam of the hunter in your eye and bring down your bird. There is no other method. You must have the urge to rummage about. You must learn to love the feel of old books; the smell of them must be unto you a delicious aroma. But at first confine your prowling—if you can—to times when your pocketbook is lean. Your resistance is apt to be very low when the exchequer overflows. You will find it much easier to stick to a one-book or one-author plan if you buy only when you are comparatively hard up."

THEODORE L. CUYLER
1822–1909

"A good book is the very essence of a good man.—His virtues survive in it, while the foibles and faults of his actual life are forgotten.—All the goodly company of the excellent and great sit around my table, or look down on me from yonder shelves, waiting patiently to answer my questions and enrich me with their wisdom.—A precious book is a foretaste of immortality."

EX LIBRIS
NORA BEATRICE
DICKSEE

D

FELIX DAHN
1834–1912

"To write books is so easy, it requires only pen and ink and the ever-patient paper. To print books is a little more difficult, because genius so often rejoices in illegible handwriting. To read books is more difficult still, because of the tendency to go to sleep. But the most difficult task of all that a mortal man can embark on is to sell a book."

ELIZABETH DALY
1878–1967

"We all have at least one book in us."

JOHN COTTON DANA
1836–1929

"The library is the one public institution which can serve as a center of pleasure and learning for all the city. To its service all can give their sympathy and aid without restraint of politics or creed, and without thought of difference in station or in culture. Recreation, good cheer, research, business, trade, government, social life, conduct, religion, all of these in every aspect can turn to books for help."

"Libraries are pleasant places. Their shelves do not lament under the wisdom they carry; they rather delight in their burdens. Their books are, like our companions, grave or gay, as nature made them. And one may believe that the great men, our fellows, who made the best of these books, rejoice mightily when words of theirs add to the happiness of any."

"For every man the book of Power is the book that, first, gives him pleasure; next, informs him, next, sets him to thinking, and next, sets him to doing."

JONATHAN DANIELS
1902–1981

"The man who reads only for improvement is beyond the hope of much improvement before he begins."

CLARENCE DARROW
1857–1938

"Some day I hope to write a book, where the royalties will pay for the copies I give away."

CHARLES DARWIN
1809–1882

"What a book a devil's chaplain might write on the clumsy, wasteful, blundering, low, and horribly cruel works of nature!"

WILLIAM DAVENANT
1605–1668

"Books shew the utmost conquests of our minds."

ROBERTSON DAVIES
1913–1995

"There are times when I think that the reading I have done in the past has had no effect except to cloud my mind and make me indecisive."

"The great sin . . . is to assume that something that has been read once has been read forever. . . . We must not gobble a work like chocolates or olives or anchovies and think we know it forever. Nobody ever reads the same book twice."

GEORGE DAWSON
1821–1876

"The man who is fond of books is usually a man of lofty thought, and of elevated opinions."

"A great library contains the diary of the human race."

"I go into my library as to a hermitage—and it is one of the best hermitages the world has. What matters the scoff of the fool when you are safely amongst the great men of the past? How little of the din of this stupid world enters into a library, how hushed are the foolish voices of the world's hucksterings, barterings, and bickerings!"

CLARENCE DAY
1874–1935

"The world of books is the most remarkable creation of man. Nothing else that he builds ever lasts. Monuments fall; nations perish; civilizations grow old and die out; and, after an era of darkness, new races build others. But in the world of books are volumes that have seen this happen again and again, and yet live on, still young, still as fresh as the day they were written, still telling men's hearts of the hearts of men centuries dead."

EUGÉNIE DE GUÉRIN
1805–1848

"Good books are the manna of the people of God, the celestial food of souls on their journey to Heaven."

EUGÈNE DELACROIX
1799–1863

"A great man's book is a compromise between the reader and himself."

THOMAS DE QUINCEY
1785–1859

"It is one of the misfortunes of life that one must read thousands of books only to discover that one need not have read them."

RENÉ DESCARTES
1595–1650

"The reading of all good books is like conversation with the finest men of past centuries."

ALEXIS DE TOCQUEVILLE
1805–1869

"In America, the majority raises formidable barriers around the liberty of opinion: within these barriers, an author may write what he pleases, but woe to him if he goes beyond them."

THEODORE L. DE VINNE
1828–1914

"Caviling with a publisher about good or bad taste is of doubtful propriety. The printer who poses as an oracle of good taste will be rated, to paraphrase Emerson's expression, as 'a typographical peacock.' "

BERNARD DE VOTO
1897–1955

"Blessed are they who read books simply because they like to. They have the amateur spirit and they get one of the few pleasures an impure world affords."

PETER DE VRIES
1910–1993

"I love being a writer. What I can't stand is the paperwork."

"I write when I'm inspired, and I see to it that I'm inspired at nine o'clock every morning."

MELVIL DEWEY
1851–1931

"The time *was* when a library was very like a museum and the librarian was a mouser in musty books. The time *is* when the library is a school and the librarian is in the highest sense a teacher, and a reader is a workman among his tools."

THOMAS F. DIBDIN
1776–1847

"I well recollect . . . glancing down [a] long list of names, my eye lit upon a work which I had long sought and yearned for. . . . For the next few days I had no thought but that one. I discoursed Nuremburg Chronicle; I ate, drank, and inhaled nothing but Nuremburg Chronicle. I dropped in at stray hours to look after its safety, and glared savagely at other parties who were turning over its leaves."

"The library of a good man is one of his most constant, cheerful, and instructive companions; and as it has delighted him in youth, so will it solace him in old age."

"A passion for books is perfectly compatible with any situation, however active and arduous."

R. A. DICK
1898–1979

" 'But what will the book be about?' said Lucy doubtfully.
'Me,' said the captain. 'It will be the story of my life—and I shall call it—I shall call it, *Blood and Swash*.' "

" 'They say every man and woman has one book in him,' said the colonial bishop. 'I wrote mine when I was ten, 'Black Ben's Booty,' it was called, and I wrote it in the Scripture class at my prep school.' "

CHARLES DICKENS
1812–1870

" 'How should you like to grow up a clever man and write books?' Oliver considered a little while . . . 'Well well,' said the old gentleman, 'Don't be afraid! We won't make an author of you while there is an honest trade to be learned, or brick-making to turn to.' "

"Mr. Gradgrind greatly tormented his mind about what people read in this library—a point whereon little rivers of tabular statements periodically flowed into the howling ocean of tabular statements, which no diver ever got to any depth in and came up sane."

"There are books of which the backs and covers are by far the best parts."

"My father had left a small collection of books in a little room upstairs, to which I had access (for it adjoined my own), and which nobody else in our house ever troubled. From that blessed little room, Roderick Random, Peregrine Pickle, Humphrey Clinker, Tom Jones, the Vicar of Wakefield, Don Quixote, Gil Blas, and Robinson Crusoe, came out, a glorious host, to keep me company. They kept alive my fancy, and my hope of something beyond that place and time,—they, and the *Arabian Nights*, and the *Tales of the Genii*—and did me no harm; for whatever harm was in some of them was not there for me; *I* knew nothing of it."

"I struggled through the alphabet as if it had been a bramble-bush; getting considerably worried and scratched by every letter."

JAMES DICKEY
1923–

"Suicide *attempts*, and then writing *poems* about your suicide attempts, is just pure bullshit!"

EMILY DICKINSON
1830–1886

"If I read a book and it makes my whole body so cold no fire can ever warm me, I know that it is poetry."

"There is no frigate like a book
To take us lands away,
Nor any coursers like a page
Of prancing poetry."

"A precious moldering pleasure 'tis
To meet an antique book,
In just the dress his century wore;
A privilege, I think,
His venerable hand to take,
And warming in our own,
A passage back, or two, to make
To times when he was young."

DENIS DIDEROT
1713–1784

"Were I to sell my library, I would keep back Homer, Moses, and Richardson."

JOAN DIDION
1934–

"I write entirely to find out what I'm thinking, what I'm looking at, what I see and what it means. What I want and what I fear."

ANNIE DILLARD
1945–

"The body of literature, with its limits and edges, exists outside some people and inside others. Only after the writer lets literature shape her can she perhaps shape literature."

ERNEST DIMNET
1869–1954

"Whoever has read the best books has acquired not only information but a method of thinking. Intelligence is as contagious as gracefulness and wit used to be in the eighteenth century."

"A book, like a landscape, is a state of consciousness varying with readers."

BENJAMIN DISRAELI
1804–1881

"An author may influence the fortunes of the world to as great an extent as a statesman or a warrior. A book may be as great a thing as a battle, and there are systems of Philosophy which have produced as great revolutions as any that have disturbed the social and political existence of our centuries."

"Read no history; nothing but biography; for that is life without theory."

"When I want to read a novel I write one."

"Books are fatal; they are the curse of the human race. Nine-tenths of existing books are nonsense, and the clever books are the refutation of that nonsense. The greatest misfortune that ever befell men was the invention of printing. Printing has destroyed education. . . ."

"An author who speaks about his own books is almost as bad as a mother who talks about her own children."

"We can not learn men from books."

". . . guanoed her mind by reading French novels."

ISAAC D'ISRAELI
1766–1848

"The delights of reading impart the vivacity of youth even to old age."

"Bibliomania, or the collecting of an enormous heap of books without intelligent curiosity, has, since libraries have existed, infected weak minds, who imagine that they themselves acquire knowledge when they keep it on their shelves."

"There is an art of reading, as well as an art of thinking, and an art of writing."

"Great collections of books are subject to certain accidents besides the damp, the worms, and the rats; one not less common is that of the *borrowers*, not to say a word of the *purloiners*."

AUSTIN DOBSON
1840–1921

"Who, without Books, essays to learn,
Draws water in a leaky urn."

WILLIAM DODD
1729–1777

"Books, dear books,
Have been, and are my comforts, morn and night,
Adversity, prosperity, at home,
Abroad, health, sickness,—good or ill report,
The same firm friends; the same refreshments rich,
And sources of consolation."

WILLIAM DONALDSON
FL. 1768

"An author passes in review at the tribunal of criticism, as a pickpocket stands a scrutiny from the constituents of the civil power."

JOHN DONNE
1573–1631

"Away thou fondling motley humorist,
Leave mee, and in this standing woodden chest,
Consorted with these few bookes, let me lye
In prison, and here be coffin'd, where I dye."

NORMAN DOUGLAS
1868–1952

"It is with publishers as with wives; one always wants somebody else's."

"Men have lost sight of distant horizons. Nobody writes of humanity, for civilization; they write for their country, their sect; to amuse their friends or annoy their enemies."

FREDERICK DOUGLASS
1817?–1895

"The frequent hearing of my mistress reading the Bible aloud, for she often read aloud when her husband was absent, awakened my curiosity in respect to this *mystery* of reading, and roused in me the desire to learn. Up to this time I had known nothing whatever of this wonderful art, and my ignorance and inexperience of what it could do for me, as well as my confidence in my mistress, emboldened me to ask her to teach me to read. With an unconsciousness and inexperience equal to my own, she readily consented, and in an incredibly short time, by her kind assistance, I had mastered the alphabet and could spell words of three or four letters."

"Filled with the determination to learn to read at any cost, I hit upon many expedients to accomplish that much desired end. The plan which I mainly adopted, and the one which was the most successful, was that of using my young white playmates, with whom I met on the streets, as teachers. I used to carry almost constantly a copy of *Webster's Spelling-Book* in my pocket, and when sent on errands, or when play time was allowed me, I would step aside with my young friends and take a lesson in spelling."

"And as I read, behold! the very discontent so graphically predicted by Master Hugh had already come upon me. I was no longer the light-hearted, gleesome boy, full of mirth and play, as when I landed in Baltimore. Light had penetrated the moral dungeon where I had lain, and I saw the bloody whip for my back, and the iron chain for my feet, and my 'good, kind' master, he was the author of my situation."

ROBERT B. DOWNS
1903–1991

"Throughout history, whenever dictators and other tyrants have wanted to suppress opposition and to kill ideas, their first thought, almost invariably, has been to destroy the books, and frequently their authors. These despots have recognized the enormous power of books and were full conscious of the explosive forces they contain."

ARTHUR CONAN DOYLE
1859–1930

"I care not how humble your bookshelf may be, nor how lowly the room which it adorns. Close the door of that room behind you, shut off with it all the cares of the outer world, plunge back into the soothing company of the great dead, and then you are through the magic portal into that fair land whither worry and vexation can follow you no more."

"Reading is made too easy nowadays, with cheap paper editions and free libraries. A man does not appreciate at its full worth the thing that comes to him without effort. Who now ever gets the thrill which Carlyle felt when he hurried home with the six volumes of Gibbon's 'History' under his arm, his mind just starving for want of food, to devour them at the rate of one a day? A book should be your very own before you can really get the taste of it, and unless you have worked for it, you will never have the true inward pride of possession."

"A man should keep his little brain attic stocked with all the furniture that he is likely to use, and the rest he can put away in the lumber room of his library, where he can get it if he wants it."

MARGARET DRABBLE
1939–

"What really annoys me are the ones who write to say, I am doing your book for my final examinations and could you please tell me what the meaning of it is. I find it just so staggering—that you're supposed to explain the meaning of your book to some total stranger! If I knew what the meanings of my books were, I wouldn't have bothered to write them."

MARIE DRESSLER
1869–1934

"I enjoy reading biographies because I want to know about the people who messed up the world."

ELIZABETH DREW
1887–1965

"The test of literature is, I suppose, whether we ourselves live more intensely for the reading of it."

JOHN DRINKWATER
1882–1937

"These book-learned fools who miss the world. . . ."

JOHN DRURY
1596–1680

"The proper charge of the library keeper is to keep the public stock of learning, which is in books and manuscripts; to increase it, and to propose it to others in the way which may be most useful unto all; his work, then, is to be a factor and trader for helps to learning, and a treasurer to keep them, and dispenser to apply them to use, or to see them well used, or at least not abused."

JOHN DRYDEN
1631–1700

"He was naturally learn'd; he needed not the spectacles of books to read Nature: he looked inwards, and found her there."

" 'Tis a vanity common to all writers, to overvalue their own productions."

> "But of all plagues, the greatest is untold,
> The book-learned wife in Greek and Latin bold,
> The critic-dame, who at her table sits,
> Homer and Virgil quotes, and wrights their writs."

HENRI PÈNE DU BOIS
1858–1906

"A book-collector whose books belonged also to his friends, even indirectly, even in a purely sentimental fashion, could not be a book-collector for a longer time than a week."

"If the mind of a man be not pure, exalted, enthusiastic; if his heart be not filled with the immense love for beauty and humanity that poets have, he may collect books, he shall not form a library."

"The book-lover is active, creative, powerful, and his distant relative, the book-collector, passive, indifferent, flaccid."

W. E. B. DU BOIS
1868–1963

"From early days I had been intrigued by books as books. In our living room I took possession of an old 'secretary' which had come down in the family and gathered together in it a number of stray volumes which I found about the house. One I distinctly remember, *Opie on Lying*. I did not read them, but they formed my library."

GEORGES DUHAMEL
1884–1966

"A library is that venerable place where men preserve the history of their experience, their tentative experiments, their discoveries, and their plans . . . in books may be found the recipes for daily living—the prescriptions for the mind and the heart."

ALEXANDRE DUMAS
1802–1870

"In general, I begin a book only when it is written."

DAPHNE DU MAURIER
1907–1989

"Every book is like a purge; at the end of it one is empty . . . like a dry shell on the beach, waiting for the tide to come in again."

ISADORA DUNCAN
1878–1927

"It has taken me years of struggle, hard work and research to learn to make one simple gesture, and I know enough about the art of writing to realize that it would take as many years of concentrated effort to write one simple, beautiful sentence."

FINLEY PETER DUNNE
1867–1936

"The first thing to have in a libry is a shelf. Fr'm time to time this can be decorated with lithrachure. But th' shelf is th' main thing."

"Th' printin'-press isn't wondherful. What's wonderherful is that annybody shud want it to go on doin' what it does."

JIMMY DURANTE
1893–1980

"Gee dat day ah read a book—someday ah'm gonna do it again!"

Wisconsin Historical Society
Founded 1849

E

JOHN EARLE
1601?–1665

"*An antiquary* . . . is one that hath the unnatural disease to be enamoured of old age and wrinkles, and loves all things as Dutchmen do cheese, the better for being mouldy and worm-eaten. . . . He loves no library, but where there are more spiders' volumes than authors', and looks with great admiration on the antique work of cobwebs. Printed books he contemns, as a novelty of this latter age, but a manuscript he pores on everlastingly, especially if the cover be all moth-eaten and the dust makes a parenthesis between every syllable."

TRYON EDWARDS
1809–1894

"My books are my tools, and the greater their variety and perfection the greater the help to my literary work."

"We should be as careful of the books we read, as of the company we keep. The dead very often more than the living."

CHARLES W. ELIOT
1834–1926

"Books are the quietest and most constant of friends; they are the most accessible and wisest of counsellors, and the most patient of teachers."

GEORGE ELIOT
1819–1880

"No story is the same to us after a lapse of time; or rather we who read it are no longer the same interpreters."

"I have the conviction that excessive literary production is a social offense. . . . Everyone who contributes to the 'too much' of literature is doing grave social injustice."

"And bad literature of the sort called amusing is spiritual gin."

"It seems to me much better to read a man's own writings than to read what others say about him, especially when the man is first-rate and the 'others' are third-rate."

"One is led to fear that a second-hand bookseller may belong to that unhappy class of men who have no belief in the good of what they get their living by, yet keep conscience enough to be morose rather than unctuous in their vocation."

T. S. ELIOT
1888–1965

"Someone said, 'The dead writers are remote from us because we know so much more than they did.' Precisely, and they are that which we know."

"I read, much of the night, and go south in the winter."

"Yes, I suppose some editors are failed writers—but so are most writers."

"Those who talk of the Bible as a 'monument of English prose' are merely admiring it as a monument over the grave of Christianity."

"A book is not harmless merely because no one is consciously offended by it."

"The most important difference between poetry and any other department of publishing is, that whereas with most categories of books you are aiming to make as much money as possible, with poetry you are aiming to lose as little as possible."

"The immature poet imitates; the mature poet plagiarizes."

HAVELOCK ELLIS
1859–1939

"It may be a foolish fancy, but I do not like drinking at those pools which are turbid from the hoofs of my fellow creatures;

when I cannot get there before the others I like to wait until a considerable time after they have left. I could not read my Catullus in peace if I had an uneasy sense that thousands of my fellow creatures were writing to the newspapers to say what a nice girl Lesbia was, and how horrid a person Gellius, condescending to approve the poet's fraternal sentiments, lamenting the unwholesome tones of his Atys."

RALPH ELLISON
1914–1994

"What one reads becomes part of what one sees and feels."

"All novels are about certain minorities; the individual is a minority."

"Good fiction is made of that which is real, and reality is difficult to come by."

CHARLES ISAAC ELTON
1839–1900

"To gain glory by means of books you must not only possess them but know them; their lodging must be in your brain and not on the bookshelf."

RALPH WALDO EMERSON
1803–1882

"Books are the best of things if well used; if abused, among the worst. They are good for nothing but to inspire."

"The colleges, while they provide us with libraries, furnish no professors of books; and I think no chair is so much needed."

"'Tis the good reader that makes the good book; in every book he finds passages which seem confidences or asides hidden from all else and unmistakably meant for his ear."

"The profit of books is according to the sensibility of the reader; the profoundest thought or passion sleeps as in a mine, until it is discovered by an equal mind and heart."

"There are not in the world at any time more than a dozen persons who read and understand Plato."

"Consider what you have in the smallest chosen library: a company of the wisest and wittiest men that could be picked out of all civil countries in a thousand years. . . . The thought which they did not uncover to their bosom friend is here written out in transparent words to us, the strangers of another age."

"There are books . . . which take rank in our life with parents and lovers and passionate experiences."

"Meek young men grow up in libraries, believing it their duty to accept the views which Cicero, which Locke, which Bacon, have given; forgetful that Cicero, Locke, and Bacon were only young men in libraries when they wrote these books."

"Some books leave us free and some books make us free."

"In the highest civilization the book is still the highest delight. He who has once known its satisfactions is provided with a resource against calamity. Angels they are to us of entertainment, sympathy, and provocation—silent guides, tractable prophets, historians, and singers, whose embalmed life is the highest feat of art; who now cast their moonlight illumination over solitude, weariness, and fallen fortunes."

"Talent alone cannot make a writer; there must be a man behind the book."

"When I read a good book . . . I wish that life were three thousand years long."

"Our high respect for a well-read man is praise enough of literature. If we encounter a man of rare intellect, we should ask him what books he reads."

"It is not observed that . . . librarians are wiser men than others."

"Many times the reading of a book has made the fortune of a man, has decided his way of life."

"All great men have written proudly, nor cared to explain. They knew that the intelligent reader would come at last, and would thank them."

"People do not deserve to have good writing, they are so pleased with bad."

"In reading there is a sort of half and half mixture. The book must be good, but the reader must also be active."

"The scholar is led by the sweet opium of reading to pallor and squalor, to anxiety and timorousness, to a life as dry and thin as his paper, to coldness and hardness and inefficiency."

"No book has worth by itself; but by the relation to what you have from many other books, it weighs."

"I suppose every old scholar has had the experience of reading something in a book which was significant to him, but which he could never find again. Sure he is that he read it there; but no one ever read it, nor can he find it again, though he buy the book, and ransack every page."

"Plenty of books, but they require good readers; the meadow is full of milk, but it needs a cow to extract it."

DESIDERIUS ERASMUS
1469–1536

"When I get a little money, I buy books; and if there is any left, I buy food and clothes."

"Be careful that you write accurately rather than much."

"By burning Luther's books you may rid your bookshelves of him, but you will not rid men's minds of him."

RICHARD P. ETTINGER
1893–1971

"A good book is a book that sells good."

JOHN EVELYN
1620–1706

"There are two reasonable fair public libraries [in Orleans], whence one may borrow a book to one's chamber, giving but a note under hand, which is an extraordinary custom, and a confidence that has cost many libraries dear."

ex
libris
Wm.
Edgar
Fisher

CHARLES B. FAIRBANKS
1827–1859

"A book is to me like a hat or coat—a very uncomfortable thing until the newness has been worn off."

GEORGE FARQUHAR
1677?–1707

"An affected modesty is very often the greatest vanity, and authors are sometimes prouder of their blushes than of the praises that occasioned them."

WILLIAM FAULKNER
1897–1962

"I am too busy writing. It has got to please me and if it does, I don't need to talk about it. If it doesn't please me, talking about it won't improve it, since the only thing to improve it is to work on it some more. I am not a literary man but only a writer. I don't get any pleasure from talking shop."

"There are no young writers worth a damn."

"A writer needs three things, experience, observation, and imagination, any two of which, at times any one of which, can supply the lack of the others."

FRANÇOIS DE SALIGNAC DE LA MOTHE FÉNELON
1651–1715

"If all the crowns of Europe were placed at my disposal on condition that I should abandon my books and studies, I should spurn the crowns away and stand by the books."

"Let your reading have a practical bearing, let it tend to the correction of your faults, reading for reading's sake is one of the worst and commonest and most unwholesome habits."

EDNA FERBER
1887–1968

"Life can't ever really defeat a writer who is in love with writing, for life itself is a writer's lover until death—fascinating, cruel, lavish, warm, cold, treacherous, constant."

"The ideal view for daily writing, hour on hour, is the blank brick wall of a cold-storage warehouse. Failing this, a stretch of sky will do, cloudless if possible."

"I sat staring up at a shelf in my workroom from which thirty-one books identically dressed in neat dark green leather stared back at me with a sort of cold hostility like children who resent their parents. Don't stare at us like that! they said. Don't blame us if we didn't turn out to be the perfection you expected. We didn't ask to be brought into the world."

"There is no denying the fact that writers should be read but not seen. Rarely are they a winsome sight."

JOHN FERGUSON
1881–1969

"It does not follow at all that a person devoted to reading is fond of books. It is often the other way: the most learned men, the most gluttonous of readers, may not have the smallest love for books."

JOHN FERRIAR
1764–1815

"What wild desires, what restless torments seize
The hapless man, who feels the book-disease!"

"The Bibliomane exclaims with haggard eye,
'No margin!' turns in haste, and scorns to buy."

GUGLIELMO FERRERO
1871–1942

"A wolfish, insatiable hunger for printed paper and reading matter is the scourge of our civilization."

LUDWIG ANDREAS VON FEUERBACH
1804–1872

"It is with books as with young girls. It is often the best, the worthiest that are left the longest on the shelf. Yet eventually someone comes who recognizes them and draws them from the darkness of seclusion into the light of a fine sphere of activity."

EUGENE FIELD
1850–1895

"We behold another advantage which the lover of books has over the lover of women. If he be a genuine lover he can and should love any number of books, and this polybibliophily is not to the disparagement of any one of that number."

"All good and true book-lovers practise the pleasing and improving avocation of reading in bed. . . . No book can be appreciated until it has been slept with and dreamed over."

"Books cannot change. A thousand years hence they are what you find them to-day, speaking the same words, holding forth the same cheer, the same promise, the same comfort; always constant, laughing with those who laugh and weeping with those who weep."

"No man can have to do with books that presently he does not love them."

"If I know one thing better than another I know this, that my books know me and love me."

HENRY FIELDING
1707–1754

"It becomes an author generally to divide a book, as it does a butcher to joint his meat, for such assistance is of great help to both the reader and the carver."

"Books, the only way of travelling by which any knowledge is to be acquired."

"He is a sagacious reader who can see two chapters before him."

"The copy that sells best will always be the best copy."

"Pity an author who is present at the murder of his works."

"Good books always survive the bad."

"No author ought to write anything besides dictionaries and spelling-books who hath not the privilege to be admitted behind the scenes of the great theatre of Nature."

"To invent good stories, and to tell them well, are possibly very rare talents, and yet I have observed few persons who have scrupled to aim at both."

SARAH FIELDING
1710–1768

"Reading is like a mirror before us."

"There is a wide difference between reading with the attention which is necessary to digest, and extract utility from writings, and skimming over the surface of authors, with the view only of filling up a chasm of time, which is not so fortunate as to be engaged to some more entertaining amusement."

DOROTHY CANFIELD FISHER
1879–1958

"Very young writers often do not revise at all. Like a hen looking at a chalk line, they are hypnotized by what they have written. 'How can it be altered?' they think. It has to be altered. You have to learn how."

EDWARD FITZGERALD
1809–1883

"I hate all big Books."

F. SCOTT FITZGERALD
1896–1940

"I've been drunk for about a week now, and I thought it might sober me up to sit in a library."

"All good writing is swimming under water and holding your breath."

"You don't write because you want to say something, you write because you've got something to say."

"An author ought to write for the youth of his own generation, the critics of the next, and schoolmasters of ever after."

S. J. ADAIR FITZ-GERALD
1859–1925

"I have no mistress but my books."

GUSTAVE FLAUBERT
1821–1880

"He loved a book because it was a book; he loved its odour, its form, its title."

"Criticism occupies the lowest place in the literary hierarchy; as regards form, almost always; and as regards 'moral value,' incontestably. It comes after rhyming games and acrostics, which at least require a certain inventiveness."

"Books are not made like children but like pyramids . . . and they're just as useless! And they stay in the desert! . . . Jackals piss at their foot and the bourgeois climb up on them."

JOHN FLORIO
1553–1625

"Reading is the best medicine for a sicke man, the best musicke for a sadde man, the best counsel for a desperate man, the best comfort for one afflicted."

SHELBY FOOTE
1916–

"A university is just a group of buildings gathered around a library."

FORD MADOX FORD
1873–1939

"Only two classes of books are of universal appeal. The very best and the very worst."

"The first thing that you have to consider when writing a novel is your story, and then your story—and then your story!"

"I have always had the greatest contempt for novels written with a purpose."

E. M. FORSTER
1879–1970

"Books have to be read (worse luck it takes so long a time). It is the only way of discovering what they contain. A few savage tribes eat them, but reading is the only method of assimilation revealed to the West."

"Creative writers are always greater than the causes that they represent."

"What is so wonderful about great literature is that it transforms the man who reads it towards the condition of the man who wrote, and brings to birth in us also the creative impulse."

"The final test for a novel will be our affection for it, as it is the test of our friends, and of anything else which we cannot define."

"One always tends to overpraise a long book because one has got through it."

"I suggest that the only books that influence us are those for which we are ready, and which have gone a little farther down our particular path than we have yet got ourselves."

"Some reviews give pain. That is regrettable, but no author has any right to whine. He was not obliged to be an author. He invited publicity, and he must take the publicity that comes along."

JOHN FOSTER
1770–1843

"A man of ability, for the chief of his reading, should select such books as he feels are beyond his own power to have produced. What can other books do for him but waste his time or augment his vanity?"

PIERRE SIMON FOURNIER
1712–1768

"After the basic necessities of life there is nothing more precious than books."

CHARLES JAMES FOX
1749–1806

"Nothing is more delightful to lie under a tree, in the summer, with a book, except to lie under a tree, in the summer, without a book."

ANATOLE FRANCE
1844–1924

"Never lend books, for no one ever returns them; the only books I have in my library are books that other fools have lent me."

"When a thing has been said and said well, have no scruple: take it and copy it. Give references? Why should you? Either your readers know where you have taken the passage and the precaution is needless, or they do not know and you humiliate them."

"We live too much in books and not enough in nature, and we are very much like that simpleton of a Pliny the Younger, who went on studying a Greek author while before his eyes Vesuvius was overwhelming five cities beneath the ashes."

ANNE FRANK
1929–1945

"If I read a book that impresses me, I have to take myself firmly in hand before I mix with other people; otherwise they would think my mind rather queer."

BENJAMIN FRANKLIN
1706–1790

"From a child . . . all the little money that came into my hands was ever laid out on books."

"Often I sat up in my room reading the greatest part of the night, when the book was borrowed in the evening and to be returned early in the morning, lest it should be missed or wanted."

"Libraries have improved the general conversation of the Americans, made the common tradesmen and farmers as intelligent as most gentlemen from other countries, and perhaps have contributed in some degree to the stand so generally made throughout the colonies in defence of their privileges."

"Read much, but not too many books."

"And now I set on foot my first project of a public nature, that for a subscription library. I drew up the proposals, . . . procured fifty subscribers of forty shillings each to begin with, and ten shillings a year for fifty years, the term our company was to continue. We afterwards obtain'd a charter, the company being increased to one hundred: this was the mother of all the North American subscription libraries, now so numerous."

"A new town in the State of Massachusetts having done me the honour of naming itself after me, and proposing to build a steeple to their meeting-house, if I would give them a bell, I have advised the sparing themselves the expense of a steeple for the present, and that they would accept of books instead of a bell, sense being preferable to sound."

"If you would not be forgotten, as soon as you are dead and rotten, either write things worth reading, or do things worth the writing."

"Nothing gives an author so much pleasure as to find his works respectfully quoted by other learned authors."

> "The Body of B. Franklin,
> Printer,
> Like the Cover of an old Book,

Its Contents torn out,
And Stript of its Lettering and Gilding,
Lies here, Food for Worms.
But the Work shall not be wholly lost:
For it will, as he believed, appear once more,
In a new and more perfect Edition,
Corrected and amended
By the Author."

ROBERT FROST
1874–1963

"I have never started a poem yet whose end I knew. Writing a poem is discovering."

"No tears in the writer, no tears in the reader."

JAMES A. FROUDE
1818–1894

"What did passengers do on long voyages when there were no novels? They must bless the man that invented them."

THOMAS FULLER
1608–1661

"It is a vanity to persuade the world one hath much learning, by getting a great library. As soon will I believe every one is valiant that hath a well-furnished armoury."

"Learning hath gained most by those books by which the printers have lost."

"To divert at any time a troublesome fancy, run to thy books; they always receive thee with the same kindness."

"A book that is shut is but a block."

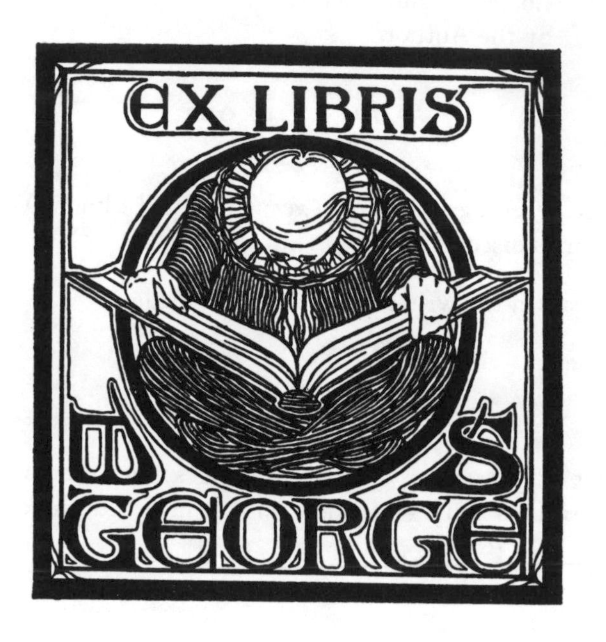
EX LIBRIS
W S
GEORGE

G

MOHANDAS K. GANDHI
1869–1948

"Real education consists in drawing the best out of yourself. What better book can there be than the book of humanity?"

JOHN GARDNER
1933–1982

"I certainly never wrote a review about a bad book, unless it's an enormously fashionable bad book."

HEATHCOTE W. GARROD
1878–1960

"All literature springs from the ineradicable instinct in man to communicate good; and thus almost all books assure us that the soul is divine."

"I call nothing a book which does not address a large part of its appeal to imagination and emotion."

"Only in the East is man polygamous; nearly everywhere he is polybiblous—a creature of many books."

MARCUS GARVEY
1887–1940

"I read *Up From Slavery* and then my dream—if I may so call it—of being a race leader dawned."

JOHN GAY
1685–1732

"Whence is thy learning? Hath thy toil
O'er books consum'd the midnight oil?"

"Variety's the source of joy below,
From whence still fresh revolving pleasures flow.
In books and love, the mind one end pursues,
And only change th'expiring flame renews.

EDWARD GIBBON
1737–1794

"From this slender beginning I have gradually formed a numerous and select collection of books, the foundation of all my works, and the best comfort of my life, both at home and abroad."

"Books are those faithful mirrors that reflect to our mind the minds of sages and heroes."

"Twenty-two acknowledged concubines and a library of 62,000 volumes attested to the variety of his [Emperor Gordianus] inclinations; and from the products which he left behind him, it appears that the former as well as the latter were designed for use rather than ostentation."

"Let us read with method, and propose to ourselves an end to what our studies may point. The use of reading is to aid us in thinking."

"A taste for books is the pleasure and glory of my life. The miseries of a vacant life are never known to a man whose hours are insufficient for the inexhaustible pleasure of study."

"Though I can part with land, I cannot part with books."

"My early and invincible love of reading, which I would not exchange for the treasures of India."

"Except some professional scholars, I have often observed that women in general read much more than men; but, for want of a plan, a method, a fixed object, their reading is of little benefit to themselves, or others."

ANDRE GIDE
1869–1951

"It is with noble sentiments that bad literature gets written."

"The poor novelist constructs his characters, he controls them and makes them speak. The true novelist listens to them and watches them function; he eavesdrops on them even before he knows them."

"To read a writer is for me not merely to get an idea of what he says, but to go off with him, and travel in his company."

JOHN GIELGUD
1904–

"It does seem to me very bad to spend months writing a book and then months constantly being asked what you meant by it."

ERIC GILL
1882–1940

"Letters are things not pictures of things."

"The title of a book is merely the thing to know it by; we have made of the title page a showing-off ground for printers and publishers. A smart title page will not redeem a dully printed book anymore than a smart cinema will redeem a slum."

CHARLOTTE PERKINS GILMAN
1860–1935

"Exciting literature after supper is not the best digestive."

NATALIA GINZBURG
1916–1991

"When I write stories, I am like someone who is in her own country, walking along streets that she has known since she was a child, between walls and trees that are hers."

GEORGE GISSING
1857–1903

"Many a time I have stood before a stall, or a bookseller's window, torn by conflict of intellectual and bodily need."

"To write—is not that the joy and privilege of one who has an urgent message for the world?"

"How the mood for a book sometimes rushes upon one, either one knows not why or in consequence, perhaps, of some most trifling suggestion. Yesterday I was walking at dusk. I came to an old farmhouse; at the garden gate a vehicle stood waiting, and I saw it was our doctor's gig. Having passed, I turned to look back. There was a faint afterglow in the sky beyond the chimneys; a light twinkled at one of the upper windows. I said to myself, *Tristam Shandy*, and hurried home to plunge into a book which I have not opened for I dare say twenty years."

"Whatever a man writes for effect is wrong and bad."

"To what end do I read and remember? Surely, as foolish a question as ever man put to himself. You read for your own pleasure, for your solace and strengthening. Pleasure, then, purely selfish? Solace which endures for an hour and strengthening for no combat? Ay, but I know, I know. With what heart should I live here in my cottage, waiting for life's end, were it not for those hours of seeming idle reading?"

"The public which reads, in any sense of the word worth considering, is very, very small."

"When I was literally starving in London, when it seemed impossible that I should ever gain a living by my pen, how many days have I spent at the British Museum, reading as disinterestedly as if I had been without a care!"

"Ah! the books one will never read again: they gave delight, perchance something more; they left a perfume in the memory; but life has passed them by forever."

WILLIAM EWART GLADSTONE
1809–1898

"Books are delightful society. If you go into a room and find it full of books—even without taking them from the shelves they seem to speak to you, to bid you welcome. They seem to tell you that they have got something inside their covers that will be good for you, and that they are willing and desirous to impart to you. Value them much."

"Book-collecting may have its quirks and eccentricities, but, on the whole, it is a vitalizing element in a society honeycombed by several sources of corruption."

ELLEN GLASGOW
1873–1945

"A good novel cannot be too long nor a bad novel too short."

"Did you ever stop to think that a writer will spend three years, or many more, on a book that the average reader will skim through in a few hours?"

"The share of the sympathetic publisher in the author's success—the true success so different from the ephemeral—is apt to be overlooked in these blatant days, so it is just as well that some of us should keep it in mind."

"But not until I was seven or more, did I begin to pray every night, 'O God, let me write books! Please, God, let me write books!' "

"Yes, I learned long ago that the only satisfaction of authorship lies in finding the very few who understand what we mean. As for outside rewards, there is not one that I have ever discovered."

"I suppose I am a born novelist, for the things I imagine are more vital and vivid to me than the things I remember."

"No one in the modern literary world is more lonely than the writer with a literary conscience."

RUMER GODDEN
1907–

"For a dyed-in-the-wool author nothing is as dead as a book once it is written."

WILLIAM GODWIN
1756–1836

"Books are the depository of everything that is honorable to man."

"He that revels in a well-chosen library, has innumerable dishes, and all of admirable flavour."

"He that loves reading, has everything within his reach. He has but to desire, and he may possess himself of every species of wisdom to judge and power to perform."

JOHANN WOLFGANG VON GOETHE
1749–1832

"Some books seem to have been written, not to teach us anything, but to let us know that the author has known something."

"The second part of the history of the world and the arts begins with the invention of printing."

"If any man wish to write a clear style let him be first clear in his thoughts; and if any would write in a noble style, let him first possess a noble soul."

"Everyone, in fact, merely reads himself out of a book; and, if he is a forceful personality, he reads himself into it."

"Beat him to death, the dog! He's a reviewer!"

EMMA GOLDMAN
1869–1940

"Publishers, theatrical managers, and critics ask not for the quality inherent in creative art, but will it meet with a good sale, will it suit the palate of the people? Alas, this palate is like a dumping ground; it relishes anything that needs no mental mastication."

OLIVER GOLDSMITH
1728–1794

"The volumes of antiquity, like medals, may very well serve to amuse the curious, but the works of the moderns, like the current coin of a kingdom, are much better for immediate use."

"In England, where there are as many new books published as in all the rest of Europe put together, a spirit of freedom and reason reigns among the people; they have been often known to act like fools, they are generally found to think like men."

"Books are necessary to correct the vices of the polite."

"I armed her against the censures of the world; showed her that books were sweet unreproaching companions to the miserable, and that if they could not bring us to enjoy life, they would at least teach us to endure it."

"I love every thing that's old: old friends, old times, old manners, old books, old wines."

"As writers become more numerous, it is natural for readers to become more indolent."

"Books teach us very little of the world."

"A book may be amusing with numerous errors, or it may be very dull without a single absurdity."

"The first time I read an excellent book, it is to me just as if I had gained a new friend: when I read over a book I have perused before, it resembles the meeting with an old one."

CHARLES E. GOODSPEED
1867–1950

"I found myself without a job in the fall of 1898. The silver lining in that cloud was the opportunity of fulfilling a long cherished desire. Now, I said, I can do what I always wished to do; I can try bookselling. The love of books had become a passion for me. I cared for them not only for their contents; I was keenly, if not too intelligently, interested in editions and publishers and the harmony of paper, type, illustrations, and binding, which leads towards perfection in bookmaking."

EDMUND WILLIAM GOSSE
1849–1928

"The earliest word I was known to utter was 'book,' laying my hand upon a specimen to show what I meant."

GÜNTER GRASS
1927–

"Even bad books are books and therefore sacred."

ROBERT GRAVES
1895–1985

"There's no money in poetry, but then there's no poetry in money either."

THOMAS GRAY
1716–1771

"Any fool may write a most valuable book by chance, if he will only tell us what he heard and saw with veracity."

"I shall be but a shrimp of an author."

"My life is like Harry the Fourth's supper of hens. *Poulet a la broche, Poulets en Ragout, Poulet en Hachis, Poulets en Fricasees.* Reading here, Reading there; nothing but books with different sauces."

THELMA GREEN
1906–

"If I couldn't read, I couldn't live."

ROBERT GREENE
1558?–1592

"Books are companions and friends and counsellors, and therefore ought to be civil, honest and discreet, lest they corrupt with false doctrine, rude manners and vicious living."

VARTAN GREGORIAN
1935–

"Libraries keep the records on behalf of all humanity . . . the unique and the absurd, the wise and fragments of stupidity."

SUTTON ELBERT GRIGGS
1872–1930

". . . it often requires more courage to read some books than it does to fight a battle."

". . . a race that does not read must ever be a laggard race."

PHILIP GUEDALLA
1889–1944

"Autobiography is an unrivalled vehicle for telling the truth about other people."

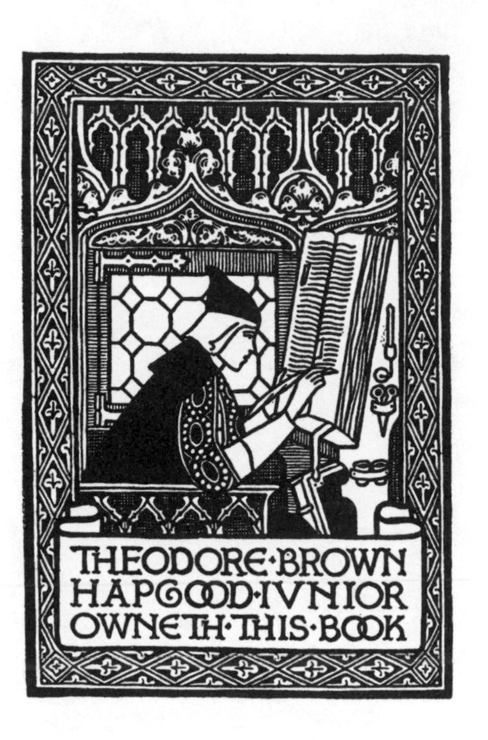
THEODORE·BROWN
HAPGOOD·IVNIOR
OWNETH·THIS·BOOK

HELEN E. HAINES
1872–1961

"I have sat through this conference waiting for someone to say that a good librarian is first of all a good bookman—a person who knows hundreds and thousands of books from having read them—a person who reads books because he loves them.

A generation of library leaders who were bookmen is passing away, and who will take their places? The education and practice of librarianship should never overlook this fundamental truth: a librarian who does not love and read books is not a good librarian."

LUCRETIA P. HALE
1820–1900

"They were sitting round the breakfast table, and wondering what they should do because the lady from Philadelphia had gone away. 'If,' said Mrs. Peterkin, 'we could only be more wise as a family!' How could they manage it? Agammemnon had been to college, and the children all went to school; but still as a family they were not wise. 'It comes from books,' said one of the family. 'People who have a great many books are very wise.' "

THOMAS C. HALIBURTON
1796–1865

"Some books are read in the parlour and some in the kitchen, but the test of a real genuine book is that it is read in both."

ROBERT HALL
1764–1831

"He might be a very clever man by nature for aught I know, but he laid so many books upon his head that his brains could not move."

"The poor man who has gained a taste for good books will in all likelihood become thoughtful; and when you have given the poor a habit of thinking you have conferred on them a much greater favour than by the gift of a large sum of money, since you have put them in possession of the principle of all legitimate prosperity."

FRANCIS WHITING HALSEY
1851–1919

"It is a universal and much-expressed regret that the literary output has of late years become almost a flood. On all sides one hears complaints of it. . . . It is now a full generation since the public began to be overwhelmed by books."

PHILIP G. HAMERTON
1834–1894

"We cannot bring ourselves to admit that the library we have collected is in great part closed to us simply by want of time. A dear friend of mine indulged in wonderful illusions about reading, and collected several thousand volumes, all fine editions, but he died without having cut their leaves."

"The art of reading is to skip judiciously. Whole libraries may be skipped these days, when we have the results of them in our modern culture without going over the ground again. And even of the books we decide to read, there are almost always large portions which do not concern us, and which we are sure to forget the day after we have read them."

"When I open a noble volume, I say to myself, 'Now the only Croesus that I envy is he who is reading a better book than this.' "

GAIL HAMILTON
1833–1896

"Whatever an author puts between the two covers of his book is public property; whatever of himself he does not put there is his private property, as much as if he had never written a word."

OSCAR HAMMERSTEIN, II
1895–1960

"There are no books like a dame."

HELEN HANFF
1916–1989

"I do love secondhand books that open to the page some previous owner read oftenest."

"Why is it that people who wouldn't dream of stealing anything else think it's perfectly all right to steal books?"

ELIZABETH HARDWICK
1916–

"The 'book'—a plaguing growth that does not itself grow, but attaches, hangs on, a tumorous companion made up of the deranged cells of learning, experience, thinking."

THOMAS HARDY
1840–1928

"My argument is that War makes rattling good history; but Peace is poor reading."

"The regular resource of people who don't go enough into the world to live a novel is to write one."

"I never care much for reading what one ought to read."

"It is only those who half know a thing that write about it."

"The real, if unavowed, purpose of fiction is to give pleasure by gratifying the love of the uncommon in human experience, mental or corporal."

AUGUSTUS W. & JULIUS C. HARE
1792–1834 1775–1855

"Reading is to the mind what exercise is to the body. It is wholesome and bracing for the mind to have its faculties kept on the stretch."

"When a man says he sees nothing in a book, he very often means that he does not see himself in it."

JOHN HARINGTON
1561–1612

"Bookes give not wisdome where none was before,
But where some is, there reading makes it more."

FREDERIC HARRISON
1831–1923

"Every reader who holds a book in his hand is free of the inmost minds of men past and present; their lives both within and without the pale of their uttered thoughts are unveiled to him; he needs no introduction to the greatest."

"The book-lover needs most to be reminded that man's business here is to know for the sake of living, not to live for the sake of knowing."

"Collecting rare books and forgotten authors is perhaps of all collecting manias the most foolish."

"[Bibliomania] seizes hold of rational beings, and so perverts them that in the sufferer's mind the human race exists for the sake of books, and not the books for the sake of the human race."

"[A man] can hardly be said to know Scott or Shakespeare, Moliere or Cervantes, when he once read them since the close of his schooldays, or amidst the daily grind of his professional life. The immortal and universal poets of our race are to be read and re-read till their music and their spirit are a part of our nature; they are to be thought over and digested till we live in the world they created for us."

LORENZ HART
1895–1943

"If they asked I could write a book
About the way you walk and whisper and look."

NATHANIEL HAWTHORNE
1804–1864

"I don't want to be a doctor, and live by men's diseases; nor a minister to live by their sins; nor a lawyer to live by their quarrels. So I don't see there's anything left for me but to be an author."

"It is a heavy annoyance to a writer, who endeavors to represent nature, its various attitudes and circumstances, in a reasonably correct outline and true coloring, that so much of the mean and ludicrous should be hopelessly mixed up with the purest pathos which life anywhere supplies to him."

DENYS HAY
1915–1994

"The printed page illuminates the mind of man and defies, as far as anything sublimary can, the corrosive hand of time."

S. I. HAYAKAWA
1906–1992

"In a very real sense, people who have read good literature have more than people who cannot or will not read. . . . It is not true that we have only one life to live; if we can read, we can live as many more lives and as many kinds of lives as we wish."

WILLIAM HAZLITT
1778–1830

"A great wit and statesman said that 'speech was given to man to conceal his thoughts.' So it might be said that books serve as a screen to keep us from a knowledge of things."

"Books are less often made use of as spectacles to look at nature with than as blinds to keep out its strong light and shifting scenery from weak eyes and indolent dispositions."

"Books are but one inlet of knowledge, and the powers of the mind, like those of the body, should be left open to all impressions."

"Reading is perhaps the greatest pleasure you will have in life; the one you will think of longest, and repent of least."

"I hate to read new books. There are twenty or thirty volumes that I have read over and over again, and these are the only ones that I have any desire ever to read at all."

LAFCADIO HEARN
1850–1904

"I cannot comfortably read a book belonging to another person because I feel all the time afraid of spoiling it."

RICHARD HEBER
1773–1833

"No gentleman can be without three copies of a book, one for show, one for use, and one for borrowers."

BEN HECHT
1893–1964

"I have tired of the look of many things, but never of books. I have kept them always in my bedroom so I could see them from my bed as I used to in this attic room. They still surround me at night, and I look at them tenderly and without thought as I fall asleep."

HEINRICH HEINE
1797–1856

"Where books are burned, human beings will in the end be burned too."

"No author is a man of genius to his publisher."

"When women write they always have one eye on the paper and the other on a man."

JOSEPH HELLER
1923–

"I can't start writing until I have a closing line."

"He knew everything about literature except how to enjoy it."

LILLIAN HELLMAN
1905–1984

"Nothing you write, if you hope to be any good, will ever come out as you first hoped."

"They're fancy talkers about themselves, writers. If I had to give young writers advice, I would say don't listen to writers talk about writing or themselves."

"Writers can be the stinkers of all time, can't they?"

ARTHUR HELPS
1813–1875

"Reading is sometimes an ingenious device for avoiding thought."

"For the lovers of ease, the delicate in health, the reserved, the fastidious and the musing, books are amongst the chief sources of delight."

CLAUDE-ADRIEN HELVÉTIUS
1715–1771

"To limit the press is to insult a nation; to prohibit reading of certain books is to declare the inhabitants to be either fools or slaves."

ERNEST HEMINGWAY
1899–1961

"The most essential gift for a good writer is a built-in shock-proof shit-detector."

"All good books are alike in that they are truer than if they had really happened and after you are finished reading one you will feel that all that happened to you and afterwards it all belongs to you; the good and the bad, the ecstasy, the remorse and sorrow, the people and the places and how the weather was."

"Writing, at its best, is a lonely life. Organizations for writers palliate the writer's loneliness, but I doubt if they improve his writing."

"All modern American literature comes from one book by Mark Twain called *Huckleberry Finn*."

"Once writing has become your major vice and greatest pleasure only death can stop it."

"When writing a novel a writer should create living people; people not characters. A character is a caricature."

"They can't yank a novelist like they can a pitcher. A novelist has to go the full nine innings, even if it kills him."

"Real seriousness in regard to writing is one of two absolute necessities. The other, unfortunately, is talent."

O. HENRY
1862–1910

"A story with a moral appended is like the bite of a mosquito. It bores you, and then injects a stinging drop to irritate your conscience."

KATHARINE HEPBURN
1909–

"What in the world would we do without our libraries?"

JOHN HERSCHEL
1792–1871

"Of all the amusements which can possibly be imagined for a hard-working man, after his daily toil, there is nothing like reading an entertaining book, supposing him to have a taste for it, and the book to read."

"If I were to pray for a taste which should stand me in stead under every variety of circumstances, and be a source of happiness and cheerfulness to me through life, and a shield against its ills, however things might go amiss, and the world frowns upon me, it would be a taste for reading."

JOHN HERSEY
1914–1993

"Journalism allows its readers to witness history; fiction gives its readers an opportunity to live it."

HERMANN HESSE
1877–1962

"Of the many things which man did not receive as a gift of nature, but which he created with his own spirit, the world of books is the greatest. . . . Without words, without writing, and without books there would be no history, there could be no concept of humanity."

GILBERT HIGHET
1906–1978

"The life of a good book is far longer than the life of a man. Its author dies, and his generation dies, and his successors are born and die; the world he knew disappears, and new orders which he could not foresee are established on its ruins; law, religion, science, commerce, society, all are transformed into shapes which would astound him; but his book continues to live. Long after he and his epoch are dead, the book speaks with his voice."

THOMAS HOBBES
1588–1679

"If I had read as much as other men, I should have been as ignorant as others."

"He that takes up conclusions on the trust of authors . . . loses his labour, and does not know anything, but only believeth."

"The praise of ancient authors proceeds not from the reverence of the dead, but from the competition and mutual envy of the living."

JOSIAH GILBERT HOLLAND
1819–1881

"There is no point where art so nearly touches nature as when it appears in the form of words."

ROBERT CORTES HOLLIDAY
1880–1947

"What is it that all men say in a book shop? The great say it, even, and the far from great. Each in his turn looks solemnly at his companion or at the salesman and says: 'Of the making of books there is no end.' Then each in his turn lights into a smile. He has said something pretty good."

HAROLD C. HOLMES
1878–1965

"Like the old miner on the Mother Lode, the antiquarian bookseller never abandons the hope of striking a rich deposit. A nugget of gold, while hidden in the earth is worthless until found by the miner, and to the finder goes the reward. Rare or unusual books are worthless while hiding in the dust of an attic, or gathering mould in the basement. Not until they are rescued from oblivion by an informed bibliophile do they eventually find a worthy repository."

OLIVER WENDELL HOLMES
1809–1894

"The best of a book is not the thought which it contains, but the thought which it suggests; just as the charm of music dwells not in the tones but in the echoes of our hearts."

"The foolishest book is a kind of leaky boat on a sea of wisdom; some of the wisdom will get in anyway."

"When Providence throws a good book in my way I bow to its decree and purchase it as an act of Piety, so long as it is reasonably or unreasonably cheap."

"What the mulberry leaf is to the silkworm, the author's book, treatise, essay, poem, is to the critical larvae that feed upon it. It furnishes them with food and clothing."

"What refuge is there for the victim who is possessed with the feeling that there are a thousand new books he ought to read, while life is only long enough for him to attempt to read a hundred."

"The first thing naturally when one enters a scholar's study or library, is to look at his books. One gets a notion very speedily of his tastes and the range of his pursuits, by a glance round his book-shelves."

"I must have my literary harem, my *parc aux cerfs*, where my favourites await my moments of leisure and pleasure,—my scarce and precious editions, my luxurious typographical masterpieces; my Delilahs, that take my head in their lap; the pleasant story-tellers and the like; the books I love because they are fair to look upon, prized by collectors, endeared by old associations, secret treasures that nobody else knows anything about; books, in short, that I like for insufficient reasons it may be, but peremptorily, and mean to like and to love and to cherish till death do us part. . . . The bookcase of Delilahs, that you have paid wicked prices for, that you love without pretending to be reasonable about it, and would bag in case of fire before all the rest."

"[Old books] are books of the world's youth, and new books are fruits of its age."

"Every library should try to be complete on something, if it were only the history of pinheads."

"There is infinite pathos in unsuccessful authorship. The book that perishes unread is the deaf mute of literature."

"Novelists and lawyers understand the art of 'cramming' better than any other persons in the world."

"I never saw an author in my life, saving perhaps one, that did not purr as audibly as a full-grown domestic cat on having his fur smoothed the right way by a skilful hand."

EDWIN PAXTON HOOD
1820–1885

"Be as careful of the books you read, as of the company you keep; for your habits and character will be as much influenced by the former as by the latter."

THOMAS HOOD
1799–1845

"My books keep me from the ring, the dogpit, the tavern, and the saloon."

HORACE
65–8 B.C.

"Let me have books, and stores for one year hence,
Nor make my life one flutter of suspense."

"Not gods, nor men, nor even booksellers have put up with poets' being second-rate."

"He has gained every point who has mixed practicality with pleasure, by delighting the reader at the same time as instructing him."

"You will get nothing written or created unless Minerva helps."

"Often must you turn your stylus to erase, if you hope to write something worth a second reading."

"The fickle population has changed its taste and burns with a craze for scribbling."

A. E. HOUSMAN
1859–1936

"This for all ill-treated fellows
Unborn and unbegot,
For them to read when they're in trouble
And I am not."

"Bibliophiles, an idiotic class. . . ."

"Good literature continually read for pleasure must, let us hope, do some good to the reader."

MAUREEN HOWARD
1930–

"I like density, not volume. I like to leave something to the imagination. The reader must fit the pieces together, with the author's discreet help."

WILLIAM DEAN HOWELLS
1837–1920

"If authors were not almost necessarily recluses, and ignorant of the ignorance about them, I don't see how they could endure it. Of course they are fated to be overwhelmed by oblivion at last poor fellows; but to see it weltering all round them while they are in the very act of achieving immortality must be tremendously discouraging."

"I was born a printer, you know. I can remember the time when I couldn't write, but not the time when I couldn't set type."

"Novelists might be the greatest possible help to us if they painted life as it is, and human feelings in their true proportion and relation, but for the most part they have been and are altogether noxious."

"You can't put a more popular thing than self-sacrifice into a novel."

"Nothing furnishes a room like books."

"Does it afflict you to find your books wearing out? I mean literally. . . . The mortality of all inanimate things is terrible to me, but that of books most of all."

ELBERT HUBBARD
1856–1915

"No book is of much importance, the vital thing is, What do you yourself think?"

"This will never be a civilized country until we expend more money for books than we do for chewing gum."

"A book on cheap paper does not convince. It is not prized, it is like a wheezy doctor with pigtail tobacco breath, who needs a manicure."

"An editor is one who separates the wheat from the chaff and prints the chaff."

VICTOR HUGO
1802–1885

"It is those books which a man possesses but does not read which constitute the most suspicious evidence against him."

"Behold a book. I will nourish with it five thousand souls—a million souls—all humanity. In the action of Christ bringing forth the loaves, here is Gutenberg bringing forth books. One sower heralds the other. . . . Gutenberg is forever the auxiliary of life."

"A library implies an act of faith."

LEIGH HUNT
1784–1859

"Yet this little body of thought that lies before me in the shape of a book has existed thousands of years, nor since the invention of the press, can any thing short of an universal convulsion of nature abolish it."

"Mankind are the creatures of books."

"Sitting last winter among my books, and walled round with all the comfort and protection which they and my fire-side could afford me,—to wit, a table of high-piled books at my back, my writing-desk on one side of me, some shelves on the other, and the feelings of the warm fire at my feet,—I began to consider how I loved the authors of those books; how I loved them too, not only for the imaginative pleasures they afforded me, but for their making me love the very books themselves, and delight to be in contact with them."

"Yon second-hand bookseller is second to none in the worth of the treasures which he dispenses."

"If fortune turns her face once more in kindness upon me before I go, I may chance, some quiet day, to lay my over-beating temples on a book, and so have the death I most envy."

"Nothing delights us more than to overhaul some dingy tome, and read a chapter gratuitously. Occasionally when we have opened some very attractive old book, we have stood reading for hours at the stall, lost in a brown and worldly forgetfulness, and should probably have read on to the end of the last chapter, had not the vendor of published wisdom offered, in a satirically polite way, to bring us out a chair—'Take a chair, sir; you must be tired.' "

KRISTIN HUNTER
1931–

"Writing is harder than anything else; at least *starting* to write is."

HENRY E. HUNTINGTON
1850–1927

"The ownership of a fine library is the surest and swiftest way to immortality."

ZORA NEALE HURSTON
1902–1960

"But certain things have seemed to me to be here as I heard the tongues of those who had speech, and listened to the lips of the books."

"Learning without wisdom is a load of books on a donkey's back."

ALDOUS HUXLEY
1894–1963

"Every man who knows how to read has it in his power to magnify himself, to multiply the ways in which he exists, to make his life full, significant, and interesting."

"Being one of Nature's non-censors, I simply cannot understand why any human being should want to prevent other responsible human beings from writing or reading what they like."

"The proper study of mankind is books."

"That was the chief difference between literature and life. In books, the proportion of exceptional to commonplace people is high; in reality, very low."

" 'Books,' he said—'books. One reads so many, and one sees so few people and so little of the world. Great thick books about the universe and the mind and ethics. You've no idea how many there are. I must have read twenty or thirty tons of them in the last five years. Twenty tons of ratiocination. Weighted with that, one's pushed out into the world.' "

"The world, you must remember, is only just become literate. As reading becomes more and more habitual and widespread, an ever-increasing number of people will discover that books will give them all the pleasures of social life and none of its intolerable tedium."

THOMAS H. HUXLEY
1825–1895

"In science, as in life, learning and knowledge are distinct, and the study of things, and not of books, is the source of the latter."

GEO·CLULOW
EX
LIBR
R·HOPE·96

I

JUDAH BEN SAUL IBN TIBBON
CA. 1120–CA. 1190

"Let your bookcases and your shelves be your gardens and your pleasure-grounds. Pluck the fruit that grows therein, gather the roses, the spices, and the myrrh. If your soul be satiate and weary, change from garden to garden, from furrow to furrow, from sight to sight. Then will your desire renew itself and your soul be satisfied with delight."

MOSES IBN EZRA
CA. 1060–1139

"I will make the wisdom of the ancients my portion,
And their books shall be the balm to my affliction."

HENRIK IBSEN
1828–1906

"One should not read to swallow all, but rather see what one has use for."

"An editor cannot always act as he would prefer. He is often obliged to bow to the wishes of the public in unimportant matters. Politics are the most important thing in life. . . ."

ELIZABETH INCHBALD
1753–1821

"Here, in the country, my books are my sole occupation; books my sure solace, and refuge from frivolous cares. Books are the calmers as well as the instructors of the mind."

WILLIAM INGE
1913–1973

" 'I used to go with a girl who read books. She joined the Book of the Month Club, and they had her reading books all the time! She wouldn't any more finish one than they'd send her another!' "

MARK H. INGRAHAM
1896–1982

"No matter how many things the word 'library' may mean elsewhere, here it is a place where books are treasured."

EUGUNE IONESCO
1912–1994

"If God exists, why write literature?
And if He doesn't, why write literature?"

RALPH IRON
1855–1920

"A thoughtful life, in which one might read and creep into the heart of books, as they can only be crept into when the wheels of the daily life are grinding soft and low."

"Books are not the same things when you are living among people. I cannot tell why, but they are dead. On the farm they would have been living things to me."

WASHINGTON IRVING
1783–1859

"The only happy author in this world is he who is below the care of reputation."

"The scholar only knows how dear these silent, yet eloquent, companions of pure thoughts and innocent hours become in the season of adversity. When all that is worldly turns to dross around us, these only retain their steady value. When friends grow cold, and the converse of intimates languishes into vapid civility and commonplace, these only continue the unaltered countenance of happier days, and cheer us with that true friendship which never deceived hope nor deserted sorrow."

"The land of literature is a fairy land to those who view it at a distance, but, like all other landscapes, the charm fades on a nearer approach, and the thorns and briars become visible. The republic of letters is the most factious and discordant of all republics, ancient or modern."

Lillian Durham Jones
A·D
Ex Libris
Frederick·Garrison·Hall

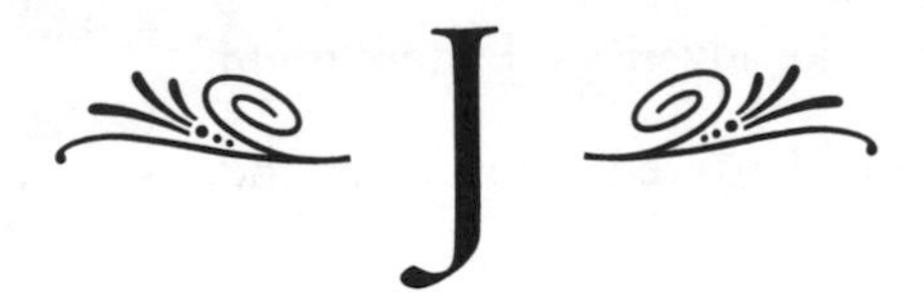

HOLBROOK JACKSON
1874–1948

"A large, still book is a piece of quietness, succulent and nourishing in a noisy world, which I approach and imbibe with 'a sort of greedy enjoyment,' as Marcel Proust said of those rooms of his old home whose air was 'saturated with the bouquet of silence.' "

"The time to read is any time: no apparatus, no appointment of time and place, is necessary. It is the only art which can be practised at any hour of the day or night, whenever the time and inclination comes, that is your time for reading; in joy or sorrow, health or illness."

"A good book is always on tap; it may be decanted and drunk a hundred times, and it is still there for further imbibement."

". . . bookmen, *men of letters*, students, and all manner of passionate readers are a species apart. . . . They become natives of a world of books, creatures of the printed word, and in the end cease to be men, as, by gradual metastasis, they are resolved into bookmen: twice-born, first of woman (as every man) and then of books, and, by reason of this, unique and distinct from the rest."

HENRY JAMES
1843–1916

"Forget not that you write for the stupid—that is, that your maximum of refinement must meet the minimum of intelligence of the audience, in other words the biggest ass it may conceivably contain."

"It takes a great deal of history to produce a little literature."

"The only reason for the existence of a novel is that it does attempt to represent life."

"I'm glad you like adverbs—I adore them."

"But then I'm a battered old novelist and it's my business to comprehend."

"The historian, essentially, wants more documents than he can really use; the dramatist only wants more liberties than he can really take."

"An enthusiasm for Poe is the mark of a decidedly primitive stage of reflection."

"Print it as it stands—beautifully."

JOHN JAY
1745–1829

"When I consider what mistakes are committed by writers on American subjects, I suspect the histories of other countries contain but very imperfect accounts of them."

"Few men have leisure or inclination to read volumes on any subject."

THOMAS JEFFERSON
1743–1826

"I cannot live without books."

"Read good books because they will encourage as well as direct your feelings."

"While residing in Paris, I devoted every afternoon I was disengaged, for a summer or two in examing all the principal bookstores, turning over every book with my own hand, and putting by everything which related to America, and indeed whatever was rare and valuable in every science."

"To the press alone, checkered as it is with abuse, the world is indebted for all the triumphs which have been gained by reason and humanity over error and oppression."

"Books constitute capital. A library book lasts as long as a house, for hundreds of years. It is not, then, an article of mere consumption but fairly of capital, and often in the case of professional men, setting out in life, it is their only capital."

"If the book be false in its facts, disprove them; if false in its reasoning, refute it. But for God's sake, let us hear freely from both sides."

"I have often thought that nothing would do more extensive good at small expense than the establishment of a small circulating library in every county, to consist of a few well-chosen books, to be lent to the people of the county, under such regulations as would secure their safe return in due time."

"From candlelight to early bedtime, I read."

"My greatest of all amusements, reading."

DOUGLAS JERROLD
1803–1857

"A blessed companion is a book—a book that, fitly chosen, is a lifelong friend . . . a book that, at a touch, pours its heart into our own."

SARAH ORNE JEWETT
1849–1909

"If you don't keep and mature your force and above all have time and quiet to perfect your work, you will be writing things not much better than you did five years ago. . . . Otherwise, what might be strength is only crudeness, and what might be insight is only observation. You will write about life, but never life itself."

JOHN OF SALISBURY
?–1180

"No iron-stained hand is fit to handle books,
Nor he whose heart on gold so gladly looks:
The same men love not books and money both,
And books thy herd, O Epicurus, loathe;
Misers and bookmen make poor company,
Nor dwell in peace beneath the same roof-tree."

DIANE JOHNSON
1934–

"The novelist, afraid his ideas may be foolish, puts them in the mouth of some other fool, and reserves the right to disavow them."

SAMUEL JOHNSON
1709–1784

"The foundation of knowledge must be laid by reading. General principles must be had from books, which, however, must be brought to the test of real life."

"Tradition is but a meteor, which, if it once fails, cannot be rekindled. Memory, once interrupted, is not to be recalled. But written learning is a fixed luminary, which, after the cloud that had hidden it has passed away, is again bright in its proper station. So books are faithful repositories, which, may be awhile neglected or forgotten, but when opened again, will again impart instruction."

"What is read with delight is commonly retained, because pleasure always secures attention; but the books which are consulted by occasional necessity, and perused with impatience, seldom leave any traces on the mind ... Books that you may carry to the fire, and hold readily in your hand are the most useful, after all.... such books form the mass of general and useful reading."

"Sir, in my early years I read very hard. It is a sad reflection, but a true one, that I knew almost as much at eighteen as I do now."

"The best part of every author is in general to be found in his book."

"I know not, madam, that you have a right, upon moral principles, to make your readers suffer so much."

"Sir, I would put a child into a library (where no unfit books are), and let him read at his choice. A child should not be discouraged from reading anything that he takes a liking to, from a notion that it is above his reach. If that be the case, the child will soon find it out and desist; if not, he of course gains the instruction which is so much the more likely to come from the inclination with which he takes up his study."

"The two most engaging powers of an author are to make new things familiar and familiar things new."

"The booksellers are generous, liberal-minded men."

"A man ought to read just as inclination leads him; for what he reads as a task will do him little good."

"One of the amusements is reading without the fatigue of close attention; and the world, therefore, swarms with writers whose wish is not to be studied, but to be read."

"No place affords a more striking conviction of the vanity of human hopes than a public library."

"People seldom read a book which is given to them. The way to spread a work is to sell it at a low price."

"People in general do not willingly read, if they can have anything else to amuse them."

"A man will turn over half a library to make one book."

"The chief glory of every people arises from its authors."

"The reciprocal civility of authors is one of the most risible scenes in the farce of life."

"I never desire to converse with a man who has written more than he has read."

"There is nothing more dreadful to an author than neglect, compared with which reproach, hatred and opposition are names of happiness."

"Read anything five hours a day, and you will soon be learned."

"Great abilities are not requisite for an historian, for in historical composition all the greatest powers of the human mind are quiescent."

CHARLES JOHNSTONE
1719?–1800?

"Who would be at the pains of writing, if it were not for the hope of making his name immortal?"

JAMES JONES
1921–1977

"Boozing does not necessarily have to go hand in hand with being a writer. . . . I therefore solemnly declare to all young men trying to be writers that they do not actually have to become drunkards first."

LEROI JONES
1934–

"Publishers are not usually very intelligent, or they might be intelligent, but it's usually hard to tell. Publishers don't publish a lot of fine books they should publish."

ERICA JONG
1942–

"Books go out into the world, travel mysteriously from hand to hand, and somehow find their way to the people who need them at the *times* when they need them. . . . Cosmic forces guide such passings-along."

"Throughout all of history, books were written with sperm, not menstrual blood."

BEN JONSON
1573?–1737

"When I would know thee, Goodyere, my thought looks
Upon thy well-made choice of friends and books;
Then do I love thee, and behold thy ends
In making thy friends books, and thy books friends."

"There must be some men are borne only to sucke out the poyson of bookes."

"Pray thee, take care, that tak'st my book in hand,
To read it well; that is, to understand."

DAVID STARR JORDAN
1851–1931

"A great library is the most important element in the formation of a great university."

PAUL JORDAN-SMITH
1885–1971

"We love books for their wisdom, their beauty, the pleasures they afford, and the comfort they give: they open doors to the only freedom we may know. Let us collect them for those reasons and no other."

MICHAEL JOSEPH
1897–1958

"Authors are easy enough to get on with—if you are fond of children."

JOSEPH JOUBERT
1754–1824

"The great drawback in new books is that they prevent our reading the old ones."

"The earliest poets and authors made fools wise. Modern authors try to make wise men fools."

"To write well one must have a natural facility and an acquired difficulty."

"Every work of genius, be it epic or didactic, is too long if it cannot be read in one day."

BENJAMIN JOWETT
1817–1893

"One man is as good as another until he has written a book."

JAMES JOYCE
1882–1941

"That ideal reader suffering from an ideal insomnia."

SYLVESTER JUDD
1813–1853

"If our hearts was only right, we shouldn't want any books."

There is no Frigate like a Book
To bear us Lands away
EX·LIBRIS
M·A·DE·WOLFE·HOWE

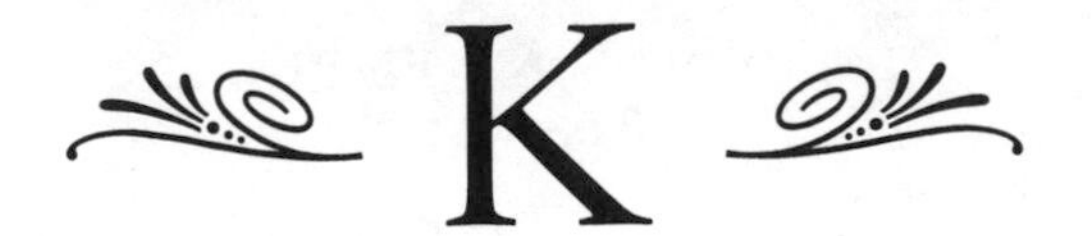

FRANZ KAFKA
1883–1924

"A book must be an ice-axe to break the seas frozen inside our souls."

ALFRED KAZIN
1915–

"It was good luck, since I wasn't much interested in anything except reading and reporting in my notebook the direct impact of everything I read."

"My pivotal experience of the raw hurting power that a book could have over me came when I first read *Oliver Twist*."

JOHN KEATS
1795–1821

"Here I possess . . . what more should I require?
Books, children, leisure . . . all my heart's desire."

"Give me books, fruit, french wine and fine weather and a little music out of doors, played by somebody I do not know."

"I am convinced more and more every day that fine writing is, next to fine doing, the top thing in the world."

"I should like the window to open onto the Lake of Geneva—and there I'd sit and read all day like the picture of somebody reading."

HELEN KELLER
1880–1868

"Literature is my Utopia. Here I am not disenfranchised. No barrier of the senses shuts me out from the sweet, gracious discourse of my book friends. They talk to me without embarrassment or awkwardness."

THOMAS À KEMPIS
1380–1471

"Everywhere I have sought rest and found it not, except sitting apart in a corner with a little book."

"If thou wouldst profit by thy reading, read humbly, simply, honestly, and not desiring to win a character for learning."

"At the Day of Judgment, we shall not be asked what we have read but what we have done."

JOHN F. KENNEDY
1917–1963

"If this nation is to be wise as well as strong, if we are to achieve our destiny, then we need more new ideas for more wise men reading more good books in more public libraries."

JOHANNES KEPLER
1571–1630

"It may be well to wait a century for a reader, as God has waited six thousand years for an observer."

COULSON KERNAHAN
1858–1943

"There are two literary maladies—writer's cramp and swelled head. The worst of writer's cramp is that it is never cured; the worst of swelled head is that it never kills."

JACK KEROUAC
1922–1969

"I wrote the book because we're all gonna die."

CHARLES KINGSLEY
1819–1875

"Except a living man there is nothing more wonderful than a book! A message to us from the dead—from human souls we never saw, who lived, perhaps, thousands of miles away."

"The men who died to buy us liberty knew that it was better to let in a thousand bad books than shut out a good one."

EDWARD N. KIRK
1802–1874

"A bad book is the worse that it cannot repent. It has long been the devil's policy to keep the masses of mankind in ignorance; but finding that they will read, he is doing all in his power to poison their books."

THE KORAN

"To each age belongeth its own Book."

JERZY KOSINSKI
1933–1991

"A writer's true calling is not about speaking, but about being 'mute,' about writing."

NIKITA KHRUSCHEV
1894–1971

"Literature plays an important role in our country, helping the Party to educate the people correctly, to instill in them advanced, progressive ideas by which our party is guided. And it is not without reason that writers in our country are called engineers of the human soul."

MILOS KUNDERA
1929–

"Ideology wants to convince you that its truth is absolute. A novel shows you that everything is relative."

JACK LONDON

L

JEAN DE LA BRUYÈRE
1645–1696

"When a book raises your spirit, and inspires you with noble and manly thoughts, seek for no other tests of its excellence. It is good, and made by a good workman."

"Making a book is a craft, as is making a clock; it takes more than wit to become an author."

"It is the glory and merit of some men to write well, and of others not to write at all."

"A man starts upon a sudden, takes Pen, Ink, and Paper, and without ever having had a thought of it before, resolves within himself he will write a Book; he has no talent at Writing, but he wants fifty Guineas."

"A mediocre mind thinks it writes divinely; a good mind thinks it writes reasonably."

"The same common sense which makes an author write good things, makes him dread they are not good enough to deserve reading."

PAUL LACROIX
1806–1884

"In personal appearance, the bookstall man partakes of the condition of his books—exposed to all the vicissitudes of the weather, sprouted and shriveled in the sun, beaten and dried by the wind, spotted and discolored by the rain. . . . The only *Manuel de Libraire* studied is the physiognomy of the purchaser: one smiles, another sighs, another knits his brows, another bites his lips; a fifth, more troubled, will finger twenty volumes before he sets his hand on the book he desires; and all betray themselves in some way which does not escape the bookstall man, who is as acute and astute as an English ambassador."

"If I were asked who is the happiest man, I would reply, a booklover. Whence it results that happiness is an old book."

CHARLES LAMB
1775–1834

"I love to lose myself in other men's minds. When I am not walking, I am reading; I cannot sit and think. Books think for me."

"I can read any thing which I call a book."

"A book reads the better, which is our own, and has been so long known to us, that we know the topography of its blots, and dog's ears, and can trace the dirt in it to having read it at tea with buttered muffins."

"There is more reason for saying grace before a new book than before dinner."

"What a place to be in is an old library! It seems as though all the souls of all the writers, that have bequeathed their labours to the Bodleians, were reposing here, as in some dormitory, or middle state. I do not want to handle, to profane the leaves, their winding-sheets. I could as soon dislodge a shade. I seem to inhale learning, walking amid their foliage; and the odour of their old moth-scented coverings is fragrant as the first block of those sciential apples which grew amid the happy orchard."

"I take less pleasure in books than before, but I like books *about* books."

"He has left off reading altogether, to the great improvement of his originality."

LOUIS L'AMOUR
1908–1988

"Begin every story in the middle. The reader doesn't care how it begins, he wants to get on with it."

WALTER SAVAGE LANDOR
1775–1864

"He who first praises a good book becomingly, is next in merit to the author."

"Clear writers, like clear fountains, do not seem so deep as they are; the turbid look the most profound."

"Every great writer is a writer of history, let him treat on what subject he may. He carries with him for thousands of years a portion of his times."

"It is dangerous to have any intercourse or dealing with small authors. They are as troublesome to handle, as easy to discourage, as difficult to pacify, and leave as unpleasant marks on you, as small children."

ANDREW LANG
1844–1912

"Broadly speaking, women detest the books which the collector desires and admires. First, they don't understand them; second, they are jealous of their mysterious charms; third, books cost money, and it really is a hard thing for a lady to see money expended on what seems a dingy old binding, or yellow paper scored with crabbed characters. Thus ladies wage a skirmishing war against booksellers' catalogues, and history speaks of husbands who have had to practice the guile of smugglers when they conveyed a new purchase across their own frontier."

"It is because the passion for books is a sentimental passion that people who have not felt it always fail to understand it."

"Book-collecting ought not to be a mere trade, or a mere fad; its object is to secure the comforts of a home for examples really rare or beautiful, or interesting as relics."

JOHN A. LANGFORD
1823–1903

"No possession can surpass, or even equal a good library, to the lovers of books. Here are treasured up for his daily use and delectation, riches which increase by being consumed, and pleasures which never cloy."

"The love of books is a love which requires neither justification, apology, nor defence. It is a good thing in itself: a possession to be thankful for, to rejoice over, to be proud of, and to sing praises for. With this love in his heart no man is ever poor, ever without friends, or the means of making his life lovely, beautiful, and happy."

"Without the love of books the richest man is poor; but endowed with this treasure of treasures, the poorest man is rich. He has wealth always increasing; possessions which the more he scatters the more they accumulate; friends who never desert him, and pleasures which never cloy."

"A wise man will select his books, for he would not wish to class them all under the sacred name of friends. Some can be accepted only as acquaintances. The best books of all kinds are taken to the heart, and cherished as his most precious possessions. Others to be chatted with for a time, to spend a few pleasant hours with, and laid aside, but not forgotten."

VALERY LARBAUD
1881–1957

"This unpunished vice, reading."

PHILIP LARKIN
1922–1985

"Get stewed: books are a lot of crap."

D. H. LAWRENCE
1885–1930

"If I *want* to write I write—and if I *don't* want to, I won't."

"If you try to nail anything down, in the novel, either it kills the novel, or the novel gets up and walks away with the nail."

" 'It satisfies my ear,' you say. Well, I don't write for your ear."

"And being a novelist, I consider myself superior to the saint, the scientist, the philosopher, and the poet, who are all great masters of different bits of man alive, but never get the whole hog."

"What is pornography to one man is the laughter of genius to another."

KATHLEEN ROCKWELL LAWRENCE
1945–

"The memory of having been read to is a solace one carries through adulthood. It can wash over a multitude of parental sins."

STEPHEN B. LEACOCK
1869–1944

"The classics are only primitive literature. They belong to the same class as primitive machinery and primitive music and primitive medicine."

FRAN LEBOWITZ
1950–

"I write so slowly, I could write with my own blood and not hurt myself."

"Having been unpopular in high school is not just cause for book publication."

"Your life would not make a good book. Don't even try."

"It's much easier to write a solemn book than a funny book. It's harder to make people laugh than to make them cry. People are always on the verge of tears."

"Contrary to what many of you might imagine, a career in letters is not without its drawbacks—chief among them the unpleasant fact that one is frequently called upon to actually sit down and write."

"Magazines all too frequently lead to books and should be regarded as the heavy petting of literature."

RICHARD LE GALLIENNE
1866–1947

"Books, those miraculous memories of high thoughts and golden moods; those magical shells tremulous with the secrets of the ocean of life, . . . those honeycombs of dreams; those orchards of knowledge; those still-beating hearts of the noble dead; . . . prisms of beauty; urns stored with all the sweets of all the summers of time; the immortal nightingales that sing for ever to the rose of life."

"The publisher is a being slow to move, slow to take in changed conditions, always two generations, at least, behind his authors."

URSULA K. LE GUIN
1929–

"The one thing a writer has to have is a pencil and some paper. That's enough, so long as she knows that she and she alone is in charge of that pencil, and responsible, she and she alone, for what it writes on that paper."

VLADIMIR ILYICH LENIN
1870–1924

"Why should freedom of speech and freedom of the press be allowed? Why should a government which is doing what it believes to be right allow itself to be criticized? It would not allow opposition by lethal weapons. Ideas are much more fatal things than guns. Why should any man be allowed to buy a printing press and disseminate pernicious opinions calculated to embarrass the government?"

ALAN JAY LERNER
1918–1986

" 'With a binding like you've got, people are going to want to know what's in the book.' "

ELIZA LESLIE
1787–1858

"Ignorant people always suppose that popular writers are wonderfully well-paid—and must be making rapid fortunes—because they neither starve in garrets nor wear rags—at least in America."

DORIS LESSING
1919–

"It does no harm to repeat, as often as you can, 'Without me the literary industry would not exist.' "

THEODOR LESSING
1872–1933

"All good books are autobiographies; but bad autobiographies are the worst of all books."

OSCAR LEVANT
1906–1972

"I've given up reading books. I find it takes my mind off myself."

DENISE LEVERTOV
1923–

"I hear the books in all the rooms
breathing calmly. . . ."

C. S. LEWIS
1898–1963

"You can't get a cup of tea large enough or a book long enough to suit me."

MATTHEW G. LEWIS
1775–1818

"Authorship is a mania, to conquer which no reasons are sufficiently strong. As easily persuade not to love as not to write."

SINCLAIR LEWIS
1885–1951

"Carol was not unhappy and she was not exhilarated, in the St. Paul Library. She slowly confessed that she was not visibly affecting lives. She did, at first, put into her contact with the patrons a willingness which should have moved worlds. But so few of these stolid worlds wanted to be moved."

"In other countries, art and literature are left to a lot of shabby bums living in attics and feeding on booze and spaghetti, but in America the successful writer or picture-painter is indistinguishable from any other decent business man."

"Our American professors like their literature clear and cold and pure and very dead."

WILMARTH S. LEWIS
1895–1979

"The following summer, in 1923, I went to England again to buy books. I had succumbed, like many amateurs in the twenties, to the fancied delights of having a share in a bookshop. Buying books was great fun; why not buy to sell and make money out of them so that I would have more money to spend on books for my own library? I was luckier than most because I got my money back."

"At this time I was nearing my twenty-eighth birthday and had about five thousand dollars a year to spend on books if I wanted to do so. . . . I was completely my own master and a born collector. The past two summers of collecting had reduced still lower my enthusiasm for my second novel, which I conscientiously pecked away at. In short, as I sat there looking at my books I was at a climacteric moment when the slightest push would make me a serious collector."

GEORGE CHRISTOPH LICHTENBERG
1742–1799

"There can hardly be a stranger commodity in the world than books. Printed by people who do not understand them; sold by people who do not understand them; criticized and read by people who do not understand them; and now even written by people who do not understand them."

"If a book and a head knock against each other and there is a hollow sound, is it always the book?"

"A book is a mirror; if a monkey peers into it, then it will not be an apostle that looks out."

"I regard reviews as a kind of infant's disease to which newborn books are subject."

A. J. LIEBLING
1904–1963

"I can write better than anybody who can write faster, and I can write faster than anybody who can write better."

JOSIAH K. LILLY, JR.
1893–1966

"In the adoption of book collecting as an avocation, I have no defense to make and no apology to offer. I recommend this intensely interesting pursuit to all who harbour the slightest inkling that it might prove pleasurable."

ABRAHAM LINCOLN
1809–1865

"For people who will like that kind of a book, that is the kind of book they will like."

ANNE MORROW LINDBERGH
1906–

"What release to write so that one forgets oneself, forgets one's companion, forgets where one is or what one is going to do next—to be drenched in sleep or in the sea. Pencils and pads are curling blue sheets alive with letters heaped upon the desk."

WALTER LIPPMAN
1889–1974

"For the newspaper is in all literalness the bible of democracy, the book out of which a people determines its conduct. It is the only serious book most people read. It is the only book they read every day."

JOHN LOCKE
1632–1704

"The reading of bad books is not only . . . standing still, but going backwards (and he that has his head filled with wrong notions is much more at a distance from the truth than he that is perfectly ignorant)."

"Those who have read of everything are thought to understand everything too; but it is not always so—reading furnishes the mind only with the materials of knowledge; it is thinking that makes what is read ours. We are of the ruminating kind and it is not enough to cram ourselves with a great load of collections; unless we chew them over again they will not give us strength and nourishment."

HENRY CABOT LODGE
1850–1924

"Here among the books we can pass out of this work-a-day world, never more tormented, more in anguish than now, and find, for a brief hour at least, happiness, perchance consolation, certainly another world and a blessed forgetfulness of the din and sorrows which surround us. Here, for the asking, the greatest geniuses will speak to us and we can rise into a purer atmosphere and become close neighbors to the stars."

JACK LONDON
1876–1919

"I write for no other purpose than to add to the beauty that now belongs to me. I write a book for no other reason than to add three or four hundred acres to my magnificent estate."

HENRY WADSWORTH LONGFELLOW
1807–1882

"The student has his Rome, his Florence, his whole glowing Italy, within the four walls of his library. He has in his books the ruins of an antique world and the glories of a modern one."

> "The love of learning, the sequestered nooks,
> And all the sweet serenity of books."

"I am never indifferent, and never pretend to be, to what people say or think of my books. They are my children, and I like to have them liked."

"Many readers judge of the power of a book by the shock it gives their feelings."

"Many critics are like woodpeckers, who, instead of enjoying the fruit and shadow of a tree, hop incessantly around the trunk pecking holes in the bark to discover some little worm or other."

"If you once understand an author's character, the comprehension of his writings becomes easy."

"He sat and bleared his eyes with books."

AMY LOWELL
1874–1925

"For books are more than books, they are the life
The very heart and core of ages past,
The reason why men lived and worked and died,
The essence and quintessence of their lives."

"All books are either dreams or swords,
You can cut, or you can drug, with words."

"Poetry and history are textbooks to the heart of man."

JAMES RUSSELL LOWELL
1819–1891

"The reading-machine always wound up and going,
He mastered what was not worth knowing."

"What a sense of security in an old book which Time has criticised for us!"

"If I were asked what book is better than a cheap book, I should answer that there is one book better than a cheap book—and that is a book honestly come by."

"For reading new books is like eating new bread,
One can bear it at first, but by gradual steps he
Is brought to death's door of a mental dyspepsy."

"I think one of the greatest pleasures is to come across a poem that one can honestly like; it is like finding a new flower."

"If one wait for the right time to come before writing, the right time never comes."

"I am a book-man."

"Have you ever rightly considered what the mere ability to read means? That it is the key which admits us to the whole world of thought and fancy and imagination? To the company of saint and sage, of the wisest and the wittiest at their wisest and wittiest moment? That it enables us to see with the keenest eyes, hear with the finest ears, and listen to the sweetest voices of all time?"

JOHN LUBBOCK
1834–1913

"We profit little by books which we do not enjoy."

"It is one thing to own a library; another to use it wisely."

CLARE BOOTH LUCE
1903–1987

"All autobiographies are alibi-ographies."

LUCIAN
CA. 120–200

"Though I am continually asking myself the question, I have never yet come to discover why you have shown so much zeal in the purchase of books. Nobody who knows you in the least would think that you do it on account of their helpfulness or use, any more than a bald man would buy a comb, or a blind man a mirror, or a deaf-mute a flute-player, or a eunuch a concubine, or a landsman an oar, or a seaman a plough."

"If Books have made you what you are, you ought of all things to avoid them."

MARTIN LUTHER
1483–1546

"The multitude of books is a great evil. There is no measure or limit to this fever for writing; every one must be an author; some out of vanity, to acquire celebrity and raise up a name; others for the sake of mere gain."

"Every great book is an action, and every great action is a book."

"The aggregation of large libraries tends to divert men's thoughts from the one great book, the Bible, which ought, day and night, to be in every one's hand. My object, my hope, in translating the Scriptures, was to check the so prevalent production of new works."

JOHN LYLY
1554?–1606

". . . far more seemly to have thy Studie full of Bookes, than thy Purse full of money."

"He that cometh in print because he would be known is like the fool that cometh into the Market because he would be seen."

EDWARD G. BULWER LYTTON
1803–1873

"Books are but waste paper unless we spend in action the wisdom we get from thought."

"In science, read by preference the newest works; in literature, the oldest. The classic literature is always modern."

"There is no Past, so long as Books shall live!"

"He who writes prose builds his temple to Fame in rubble; he who writes verse builds it in granite."

"It is not study alone that produces a writer; it is intensity."

"It is one thing to write and another to publish."

"I only wish for such readers as give themselves heart and soul up to me."

BOWDOIN COLLEGII SIGILLVM 1794
HARRIS
EX · LIBRIS
DONALD
BAXTER
MACMILLAN

M

ROSE MACAULAY
1889–1958

"It was a good book to kill time for those who like it better dead."

"He felt about books as doctors feel about medicines, or managers about plays—cynical but hopeful."

"Only one hour in the normal day is more pleasurable than the hour spent in bed with a book before going to sleep, and that is the hour spent in bed with a book after being called in the morning."

THOMAS B. MACAULAY
1800–1859

"If anybody would make me the greatest king that ever lived, with palaces and gardens, and fine dinners, and wine and coaches, and beautiful clothes, and hundreds of servants, on condition that I would not read books, I would not be a king—I would rather be a poor man in a garret with plenty of books than a king who did not read."

"Man should treasure books because—they have guided him to truth; they have filled his mind with noble and graceful images; they stood by him in all vicissitudes, comforters in sorrow, nurses in sickness, companions in solitude."

"Books are becoming everything to me. If I had at this moment any choice of life, I would bury myself in one of those immense libraries . . . and never pass a waking hour without a book before me."

"I have no pleasure from books, which equals that of reading over for the hundredth time great productions which I almost know by heart."

"Even now, I dare not, in the intervals of business, remain alone for a minute without a book in my hand."

"I have my eye on all the book-stalls, and I shall no longer suffer you, when we walk together in London, to drag me past them as you used to do."

"I met Sir Bulwer Lytton. He is anxious about some scheme for some association of literary men. I detest all such associations. I hate the notion of gregarious authors. The less we have to do with each other the better."

MARY MCCARTHY
1912–1989

"In any work that is truly creative, I believe, the writer cannot be omniscient in advance about the effects that he proposes to produce. The suspense of a novel is not only in the reader, but in the novelist, who is intensely curious about what will happen to the hero."

"An interviewer asked me what book I thought best represented the modern American woman. All I could think of to answer was: Madame Bovary."

GEORGE MACDONALD
1824–1905

"As you grow ready for it, somewhere or other you will find what is needful for you in a book."

WILLIAM MCFEE
1881–1966

"To one whose business is with books there can be nothing more alluring than the contemplation at very close range of that astonishing phenomenon by which we all live—the Public. A course of salesmanship in a bookshop would modify that austere attitude of many authors toward their publishers and the distributors of their books who, it appears upon investigation, have virtues of their own, and difficulties which do not confront the authors."

PHYLLIS MCGINLEY
1905–1978

"Run as we may, we must still read."

"There are some books one needs maturity to enjoy just as there are books an adult can come upon too late to savor."

NICCOLO MACHIAVELLI
1469–1527

"When evening has arrived, I return home, and go into my study . . . I pass into the antique courts of ancient men, where, welcomed lovingly by them, I feed upon the food which is my own, and for which I was born. Here, I can speak with them without show, and they respond to me by virtue of their humanity. For hours together, the miseries of life no longer annoy me; I forget every vexation; I do not fear poverty; altogether transferred myself to those with whom I hold converse."

ALISTAIR MACLEAN
1922–1987

"Sex? No time for it. Gets in the way of the action."

ARCHIBALD MACLEISH
1892–1982

"Keepers of books, keepers of print and paper on the shelves, librarians are keepers also of the records of the human spirit—the records of men's watch upon the world and on themselves."

"The essential is not to think of one's self as a writer and to do nothing which will put one's self in that popinjay attitude. You don't write as a writer, you write as a man."

DOUGLAS C. MCMURTRIE
1888–1944

"I believe in good book decoration, sparingly but feelingly used, and in putting more into books than the bare demands of fitness to purpose. Sound in kind and right in measure, decoration will add to the beauty of books in everyday use. It will make them more worthy the attention of those accustomed to high standards of artistry in other objects of daily use. It will make them more pleasing to read. It will sell more books."

NORMAN MAILER
1923–

"A really good style comes only when a man has become as good as he can be. Style is character."

BERNARD MALAMUD
1914–1986

"Nobody can tell a writer what can or ought to be done, or not done, in his fiction. A living death if you fall for it."

"I want the books to speak for themselves. You can read? All right, tell me what my books mean. Astonish me."

"I'm an American, I'm a Jew, and I write for all men. A novelist has to, or he's built himself a cage."

"The novel could disappear, but it won't die. . . . Those who say the novel is dead don't write them."

"First drafts are for learning what your novel or story is about. Revision is working with that knowledge to enlarge and enhance an idea, to re-form it. . . . Revision is one of the true pleasures of writing."

STÉPHANE MALLARMÉ
1842–1898

"The world was made for nothing more than to produce a beautiful book."

"The flesh, alas, is wearied; and I have read all the books there are."

HORACE MANN
1796–1859

"A house without books is like a room without windows. No man has a right to bring up his children without surrounding them with books, if he has the means to buy them. It is a wrong to his family. Children learn to read by being in the presence of books. The love of knowledge comes with reading and grows upon it."

"Every school boy and school girl who has arrived at the age of reflection ought to know something about the history of the art of printing."

KATHERINE MANSFIELD
1888–1923

"The pleasure of all reading is doubled when one lives with another who shares the same books."

"Looking back, I imagine I was always writing. Twaddle it was too. But far better to write twaddle or anything, anything, than nothing at all."

"I have discovered that I cannot burn the candle at one end and write a book with the other."

"Yes, for the last two weeks I have written scarcely anything. I have been idle; I have *failed*."

EDWIN MARKHAM
1852–1940

"He fed his spirit with the bread of books,
And slaked his thirst at all the wells of thought."

CHRISTOPHER MARLOW
1564–1593

"Ugly hell, gape not! come not, Lucifer!
I'll burn my books!"

JOHN P. MARQUAND
1893–1960

"If you have one strong idea, you can't help repeating it and embroidering it. Sometimes I think that authors should write one novel and then be put in a gas chamber."

GABRIEL GARCÍA MÁRQUEZ
1928–

"One of the most difficult things is the first paragraph. I have spent many months on a first paragraph, and once I get it, the rest just comes out very easily. In the first paragraph you solve most of the problems with your book."

DON MARQUIS
1878–1937

"Publishing a volume of verse is like dropping a rose petal down the Grand Canyon and waiting for the echo."

"Three or four years ago we made a suggestion to the Poetry Society of America to the effect that it would be a good idea for poets and editors and publishers to abstain from producing and printing any poetry for the space of five years. We wished to see if the tone of national life would not be perceptibly raised at the end of that time. But the plan was received with silence."

GEORGE PERKINS MARSH
1801–1882

"A thoughtful poem, a profound and learned history, a philosophical exposition and defence of some great truth, shall lie uncalled-for, and moulder on the publisher's shelves, while a sketchy volume, hastily scribbled in the idle intervals between the laborious diversions of a fashionable watering-place, a 'mere compound of brain-dribble and printer's ink,' shall yield a profit that will enable its author to buy a German principality or a seat in Parliament, or to build a cotton factory or a mile of railroad."

MARTIAL
CA. 40–CA. 104

"The readers and the hearers like my books,
And yet some writers cannot them digest;
But what care I? for when I make a feast,
I would my guests should praise it, not the cooks."

"Do you wonder, Theodorus, why it is that, despite your entreaties, I have never given you my books? I have an excellent reason: lest you should give me yours."

"My foolish parents taught me to read and write."

ANDREW MARVELL
1621–1678

"O printing! How hath thou disturbed the peace of mankind! That lead when molded into bullets is not so mortal as when founded into letters."

GROUCHO MARX
1891–1977

"From the moment I picked your book up until I laid it down I was convulsed with laughter. Someday I intend reading it."

"Outside of a dog, a book is man's best friend; inside of a dog, it's too dark to read."

JOHN MASEFIELD
1878–1957

"I seek few treasures, except books, the tools
Of those celestial souls the world calls fools."

COTTON MATHER
1663–1728

"In books a prodigal, they say,
A living cyclopedia."

W. SOMERSET MAUGHAM
1874–1965

"The crown of literature is poetry. . . . The writer of prose can only step aside when the poet passes."

"The four greatest novelists the world has ever known, Balzac, Dickens, Tolstoy, and Dostoyevsky, wrote their respective languages very indifferently. It proves that if you can tell stories, create character, devise incidents, and if you have sincerity and passion, it doesn't matter a damn how you write."

"Women will write novels to while away their pregnancies; bored noblemen, axed officers, retired civil servants fly to the pen as one might fly to the bottle. There is an impression abroad that everyone has it in him to write a book; but if by this is implied a good book the impression is false."

"It is astonishing how many books I find there is no need for me to read at all."

"Poor Henry [James], he's spending eternity wandering round and round a stately park and the fence is just too high for him to peep over and they're having tea just too far for him to hear what the countess is saying."

"There are three rules for writing the novel. Unfortunately, no one knows what they are."

"The only important thing in a book is the meaning it has for you."

"A good style should show no sign of efforts. What is written should seem a happy accident."

"The trouble with our younger writers is that they are all in their sixties."

"I have never met an author who admitted that people did not buy his book because it was dull."

"I would sooner read a time-table or a catalogue than nothing at all. They are much more entertaining than half the novels that are written."

ANDRÉ MAUROIS
1885–1967

"I cannot imagine a pleasanter old age than one spent in the not too remote country where I could reread and annotate my favorite books."

"In literature, as in love, we are astonished at what is chosen by others."

HERMAN MELVILLE
1819–1891

"To produce a mighty book, you must choose a mighty theme. No great and enduring volume can ever be written on the flea, though many there be that have tried it."

"The fight of all fights is to write."

"You books must know your places."

H. L. MENCKEN
1880–1956

"There are people who read too much: the bibliobibuli. I know some who are constantly drunk on books, as other men are drunk on whiskey or religion. They wander through this most diverting and stimulating of worlds in a haze, seeing nothing and hearing nothing."

"The chief knowledge that a man gets from reading books is the knowledge that very few of them are worth reading."

"The impulse to create beauty is rather rare in literary men. . . . Far ahead of it comes the yearning to make money."

"But I became a writer all the same, and shall remain one until the end of the chapter, just as a cow goes on giving milk all her life, even though what appears to be her self-interest urges her to give gin."

"A great literature is chiefly the product of inquiring minds in revolt against the immovable certainties of the nation."

"An author, like any other so-called artist, is a man in whom the normal vanity of all men is so vastly exaggerated that he finds it a sheer impossibility to hold it in."

"As a book-worm I have got so used to lewd and lascivious books that I no longer notice them. The most virtuous lady novelists write things that would have made a bartender blush two decades ago."

"Character in decay is the theme of the great bulk of superior fiction."

"In the main there are two sorts of books; those that no one reads, and those that no one ought to read."

GEORGE MEREDITH
1828–1909

"Having one's name to a volume of poems is as bad as to an advertising pill."

"All attestation favors the critical dictum that a novel is to give us copious sugar and no cane."

PROSPER MÉRIMÉE
1803–1870

"In history I love only the anecdotes."

GRACE METALIOUS
1924–1964

"If I'm a lousy writer, then a lot of people have got lousy taste."

JAMES A. MICHENER
1907–

"In the unbroken chain of which I am a part, reading breeds writing, which breeds more reading. I have grave suspicions about young writers I meet who aspire to a life in the verbal arts without having done their homework in Balzac and Camus, Tolstoy and Pasternak, Dickens and Hardy, Melville and Cheever. How can they possibly evolve the standards which will allow them to compete?"

EDNA ST. VINCENT MILLAY
1892–1950

"A person who publishes a book appears wilfully in public with his pants down."

ARTHUR MILLER
1915–

"Criticism hurt me when I had failures. I thought: I'll never write another play: But I'm an alligator. Only the alligators remain. The others get out of the water."

HENRY MILLER
1891–1980

"We should read to give our souls a chance to luxuriate."

"I have not read nearly as much as the scholar, the bookworm, or even the 'well-educated' man—yet I have undoubtedly read a hundred times more than I should have read for my own good."

"A man with his belly full of the classics is an enemy of the human race."

"No man would set a word down on paper if he had the courage to live out what he believed in."

"One thing is certain today—the illiterates are definitely not the least intelligent among us."

A. A. MILNE
1882–1956

"Almost anyone can be an author; the business is to collect money and fame from this state of being."

"My spelling is Wobbly. It's good spelling but it Wobbles, and letters get in the wrong place."

JOHN MILTON
1608–1674

"A good book is the precious life-blood of a master spirit, embalmed and treasured up on purpose to a life beyond life."

"A wise man will make better use of an idle pamphlet than a fool will do of sacred Scripture."

"If we think to regulate printing thereby to rectify manners, we must regulate all recreations and pastimes, all that is delightful to man. . . ."

"Deep verst in books and shallow in himself."

"As well almost kill a man, as kill a good book; for the life of the one is but a few short years, while that of the other may be for ages.—Who kills a man kills a reasonable creature, God's image; but he who destroys a good book kills reason itself; kills as it were, the image of God."

"A wise man, like a good refiner, can gather gold out of the drossiest volume."

"I was so allured to read that no recreation came to me better welcome."

MARIA MITCHELL
1818–1889

"A book is a very good institution! To read a book, to think it over, and to write out notes is a useful exercise; a book which will not repay some hard thought is not worth publishing."

"Let us secure not such books as people want, but books just above their wants, and they will reach up to take what is put out for them."

NANCY MITFORD
1904–1973

"I have only ever read one book in my life, and that is *White Fang*. It's so frightfully good I've never bothered to read another."

WILSON MIZNER
1876–1933

"If you copy from one author it's plagiarism. If you copy from two, it's research."

MOHAMMED
CA. 570–632

"The ink of the scholar is more sacred than the blood of the martyr."

MOLIÈRE
1622–1673

"Reading goes ill with the married state."

"The only people who can be excused for letting a bad book loose on the world are the poor devils who have to write for a living!"

"Anyone may be an honorable man, and yet write verse badly."

"All that is not prose is verse; and all that is not verse is prose."

ADRIENNE MONNIER
1892–1955

". . . in the country of books where I dwell, the dead can count entirely as much as the living."

MARY WORTLEY MONTAGUE
1689–1762

"No entertainment is so cheap as reading, nor any pleasure so lasting."

"The active scenes are over at my age. I indulge, with all the art I can, my taste for reading. If I would confine it to valuable books, they are almost as rare as valuable men. I must be content with what I can find."

MICHEL DE MONTAIGNE
1553–1592

"The mind nauseates at the thought of processions of learned dunces and dullards . . . popes of knowledge, wise fools, tyrants of information who are crammed full of learning but lifeless, stupid, repellent; men who have piled such a load of books on their heads that their brains have seemed squashed by them."

"I love no books but such as are pleasant and easy, and which tickle me, or such as comfort and counsel me, to direct my life and death."

"To gain distraction from troublesome thoughts, I have only to take refuge in books."

"There are more books upon books than upon all other subjects."

"Idle books get born because people don't attend to their proper business, but leap at the chance to divert themselves from it."

"Sometimes I read a book with pleasure, and detest the author."

"Every abridgment of a good book is a stupid abridgment."

"He that I am reading seems always to have the most force."

"The middle sort of historians, of which the most part are, they spoil all; they will chew our meat for us."

CHARLES DE SECONDAT MONTESQUIEU
1689–1755

"The love of reading a good book enables a man to exchange the wearisome hours of life, which come to everyone, for hours of delight."

LUCY MAUDE MONTGOMERY
1874–1942

"The p'int of good writing is knowing when to stop."

GEORGE MOORE
1852–1933

"If good books did good, the world would have been converted long ago."

"A book's first life, it is true, depends upon its contents, but two or three years after publication the pagination, the print, the paper, the cover, and the shape of the book begin to attract, and year by year they attract more and more until the book attains the glory of a Chinese vase in which there is nothing but a little dust."

"I was born, I live, I shall die a peculiar man. . . . I wrote the first serious novels in English. I invented adultery, which didn't exist in the English novel till I began writing."

"The one invincible thing is a good book; neither malice nor stupidity can crush it."

"A quotation, a chance word heard in an unexpected quarter, puts me on the trail of the book destined to achieve some intellectual advancement in me."

MARIANNE MOORE
1887–1972

"Any writer overwhelmingly honest about pleasing himself is almost sure to please others."

"A writer is unfair to himself when he is unable to be hard on himself."

THOMAS MOORE
1779–1852

"My only books
Were women's looks
And folly's all they've taught me."

HANNAH MORE
1745–1833

"Captious critics cut up their authors into chops, and by adding a little crumbled bread of their own, and tossing it up a little, present it as a fresh dish; you are to dine upon a poet;—the critic supplies the garnish."

"He lik'd those literary cooks
Who skim the cream of others' books;
And ruin half an author's graces
By plucking bon-mots from their places."

"We do not so much want books for good people, as books which will make bad people better."

CHRISTOPHER MORLEY
1890–1957

"Lord! When you sell a man a book you don't sell just twelve ounces of paper and ink and glue—you sell him a whole new life. Love and friendship and humour and ships at sea by night—there's all heaven and earth in a book, a real book."

"There is no mistaking a real book when one meets it. It is like falling in love, and like that colossal adventure it is an experience of great social import. Even as the tranced swain, the booklover yearns to tell others of his bliss. He writes letters about it, adds it to the postscript of all manner of communications, intrudes it into telephone messages, and insists on his friends writing down the title of the find. Like the simple-hearted betrothed, once certain of his conquest, 'I want you to love her, too!' It is a jealous passion also. He feels a little indignant if he finds that anyone else has discovered the book also.... There are even some perversions of passion by which a booklover loses much of his affection for his pet if he sees it too highly commended by some rival critic."

"There are some knightly souls who ... make their visits to bookshops ... not because they need any certain volume, but because they feel that there may be some book that needs them.... Some wistful, little forgotten sheaf of loveliness, long pining away on an upper shelf—why not ride up, fling her across your charger (or your charge account) and gallop away. Be a little knightly, you booklovers!"

JOHN MORLEY
1838–1923

"There are some books which cannot be adequately reviewed for twenty or thirty years after they come out."

JAN MORRIS
1926–

"When things get too awful, when the rain never seems likely to stop, and the toolmakers are striking, and Sam the dog has been rolling in manure—when life seems irredeemable, then I retreat to the lost world of my own guide-books."

WILLIAM MORRIS
1834–1896

"If I were asked to say what is at once the most important production of Art and the thing most to be longed for, I should answer, A beautiful House; and if I were further asked to name the production next in importance and the thing next to be longed for, I should answer, A beautiful Book. To enjoy good houses and good books in self-respect and decent comfort, seems to me to be the pleasurable end towards which all societies of human beings ought now to struggle."

"I began printing books with the hope of producing some which would have a definite claim to beauty, while at the same time they should be easy to read and should not dazzle the eye, or trouble the intellect of the reader by eccentricity of form in the letters."

TONI MORRISON
1931–

"I write the kind of books I want to read."

"I write the way women have babies. You don't know it's going to be like that. If you did, there's no way you would go through with it."

PERCY H. MUIR
1894–1979

"The common books you may pick up at leisure, rarities must be seized whenever they occur, for you may not see them again, for a long time, and by then the price may have risen against you."

FRANK ARTHUR MUMBY
1872–1954

"To write a book is a task needing only pen, ink and paper; to print a book is more difficult, because genius often expresses itself illegibly; to read a book is more difficult still, for one has to struggle with sleep; but to sell a book is the most difficult task of all."

From the Books of
GILBERT NORTH
"A Good
BooK is
the Best of
Friends,
the Same
To-day and
Forever"
Martin Tupper

VLADIMIR NABOKOV
1899–1977

"Literature was not born the day when a boy crying 'wolf, wolf' came running out of the Neanderthal valley with a big gray wolf at his heels; literature was born on the day when a boy came crying 'wolf, wolf' and there was no wolf behind him."

"Style and structure are the essence of a book; great ideas are hogwash."

V. S. NAIPAUL
1932–

"I am the kind of writer that people think other people are reading."

NAPOLEON I
1769–1821

"[As a young man] I lived alone like a hermit, in a little room with my books—then my only friends. What strict economy it required even in the necessaries of life before I could allow myself the pleasure of purchasing them! When I had managed to save up two crowns by dint of stern self-denial, I wended my way to the bookseller's as pleased as a child, and I examined his shelves long and anxiously before my purse would allow me to gratify my desires."

"God, how stupid literary men are!"

"Since the discovery of printing, knowledge has been called to power, and power has been used to make knowledge a slave."

GEORGE JEAN NATHAN
1882–1958

"There is no such thing as a dirty theme. There are only dirty writers."

GLORIA NAYLOR
1950–

"One should be able to return to the first sentence of a novel and find the resonances of the entire work."

EDITH NESBITT
1858–1924

"I ought to have put this in the preface, but I never read prefaces, and it is not much good writing things just for people to skip. I wonder other writers have never thought of this."

JOHN HENRY NEWMAN
1801–1890

"How much more profitable for the independent mind, after the mere rudiments of education, to range through a library at random, taking down books as they meet him, and pursuing the trains of thought which his mother wit suggests!"

A. EDWARD NEWTON
1863–1940

"Even when reading is impossible, the presence of books acquired (by passionate devotion to them) produces such an ecstasy that the buying of more books than one can peradventure read is nothing less than the soul reaching towards infinity. . . . We cherish books even if unread, their mere presence exudes comfort, their ready access, reassurance."

"Books are for me a solace and a joy. We are told that of the making of them there is no end. Be it so. Let us rejoice that, whatever comes, books will continue to be, books that suit our every mood and fancy. If all is vanity, as 'The Preacher' says, how can we better employ our time than by reading books and writing about them?"

"The one best and sufficient reason for a man to buy a book is because he thinks he will be happier with it than without it."

"Better men than I have parted with their books, better men, mind you, but none with a greater love than I; and if my present collection has to be jettisoned, I'll at once begin collecting over again."

JOHN B. NICHOLSON, JR.
1912–

"I never enter a large library when it is quiet and deserted that I am not aware of a restless vitality which seems to permeate its atmosphere, and I am convinced that this restlessness is nothing more or less than the spirited will of great books to draw the reader into the marvelous world of the printed page, where there are no prisons for the mind but only great expanses of a brightly lighted kingdom, where the riches of the Indies are laid out for any who would seek them."

"Books are for me symbols of such real pleasure that even being aware of their presence in a room brings contentment."

FRIEDRICH NIETZSCHE
1844–1900

"Of all that has been written, I love only that which was written in blood."

"No one can draw more out of things, books included, than he already knows, A man has no ears for that to which experience has given him no access."

"It is my ambition to say in ten sentences what other men say in whole books—what other men do not say in whole books."

"Books for all the world are always foul-smelling books: the smell of small people clings to them."

"A book calls for pen, ink, and a writing desk; today the rule is that pen, ink, and a writing desk call for a book."

"A book is made better by good readers and clearer by good opponents."

ANAÏS NIN
1903–1977

"The role of a writer is not to say what we all can say, but what we are unable to say."

"We write to taste life twice, in the moment and in retrospection."

KWAME NKRUMAH
1902–1977

"Of all the literature that I studied, the book that did more than any other to fire my enthusiasm was the *Philosophy and Opinions of Marcus Garvey*."

ALBERT JAY NOCK
1873–1945

"As sheer casual reading-matter, I still find the English dictionary the most interesting book in our language."

KATHLEEN NORRIS
1880–1966

"There seems to be no physical handicap or chance of environment that can hold a real writer down, and there is no luck, no influence, no money that will keep a writer going when she is written out."

"Just the knowledge that a good book is awaiting one at the end of a long day makes that day happier."

JOHN NORRIS
1657–1711

"Reading without thinking, may indeed make a rich commonplace, but twill never make a clear head."

THOMAS NORTH
1535?–1601?

"For men that read much and work little are as bells, the which do sound to call others, and they themselves never enter into the church."

ELEANOR HOLMES NORTON
1937–

"It's difficult to beat making *your* living thinking and writing about subjects that matter to you."

Ex Libris
Elizabeth Langdon

O

JOYCE CAROL OATES
1938–

"Man is a problem-solving animal and the organizing of vast subjects must give pleasure, evidently; nothing seems to me to involve more intellectual effort than the organizing of a big novel, and I cannot imagine anything more rewarding."

"I am inclined to think that as I grow older I will come to be infatuated with the art of revision, and there may come a time when I will dread giving up a novel at all."

FLANNERY O'CONNOR
1925–1964

"Everywhere I go, I'm asked if the universities stifle writers. My opinion is that they don't stifle enough of them. There's many a best seller that could have been prevented by a good teacher."

"Elizabeth Hardwick told me once that all her first drafts sounded as if a chicken had written them. So do mine for the most part."

"Writing is a good example of self-abandonment. I never completely forget myself except when I am writing and I am never more completely myself than when I am writing."

JOHN O'HARA
1905–1970

"Hot lead can be almost as effective coming from a linotype as from a firearm."

TILLIE OLSEN
1913–

"Writers in a profit making economy are an exploitable commodity whose works are products to be marketed, and are so judged and handled."

"Literature is a place for generosity and affection and hunger for equals—not a prizefight ring. We are increased, confirmed in our medium, roused to do our best, by every good writer, every fine achievement. Would we want one good writer or fine book less?"

"Every woman who writes is a survivor."

WILLIAM DANA ORCUTT
1870–1953

"My library has taken on a different aspect during all these years. When I first installed my books I looked on it as a sanctuary, into which I could escape from the world outside. . . . My library has lost none of that blissful peace as a retreat, but in addition it has become a veritable meeting ground. The authors I have known are waiting for me there,—to disclose to me through their works far more than they, in all modesty, would have admitted in our personal conferences."

"A book in itself is always something more than paper and type and binder's boards. It possesses a subtle friendliness that sets it apart from other inanimate objects about us, and stamps it with an individuality which responds to our approach in proportion to our interest."

P. J. O'ROURKE
1947–

"Don't read science fiction books. It'll look bad if you die in bed with one on the nightstand. Always read stuff that will make you look good if you die in the middle of it."

JOSÉ ORTEGA Y GASSET
1883–1955

"If each new generation continues to accumulate printed paper in the same proportion as the last few generations, the problem posed by the excess of books will become truly terrifying. The culture which has liberated man from the primitive forests now thrusts him anew into the midst of a forest of books no less inextricable and stifling."

GEORGE ORWELL
1903–1950

"All writers are vain, selfish and lazy, and at the very bottom of their motives lies a mystery. Writing a book is a long, exhausting struggle, like a long bout of some painful illness. One would never undertake such a thing if one were not driven by some demon one can neither resist nor understand."

"The existence of good bad literature—the fact that one can be amused or excited or even moved by a book that one's intellect refuses to take seriously—is a reminder that art is not the same thing as cerebration."

"Prolonged, indiscriminate reviewing of books involves constantly inventing reactions towards books about which one has no spontaneous feelings whatever."

FRANCIS OSBORNE
1593–1639

"A few books thoroughly digested, rather than hundreds but gargled in the mouth. . . ."

WILLIAM OSLER
1848–1919

"With half an hour's reading in bed every night as a steady practice, the busiest man can get a fair education before the plasma sets in the periganglionic spaces of his grey cortex."

OVID
43 B.C.?–17 A.D.

"While writing the very toil gives pleasure, and the growing work glows with the writer's heart."

EX LIBRIS
RS
PAGE

THOMAS PAINE
1737–1809

"A man may write himself out of reputation when nobody else can do it."

"A Magazine when properly conducted, is the nursery of genius; and by constantly accumulating new matter, becomes a kind of market for wit and utility."

"The connection between vice and meanness is a fit object for satire, but when the satire is a fact, it cuts with the irresistible power of a diamond."

"The art of printing changes all the cases, and opens a scene as vast as the world. It gives to man a sort of divine attribute. It gives to him mental omnipresence. He can be everywhere and at the same instant; for wherever he is read he is mentally there."

"Universal empire is the prerogative of a writer. His concerns are with all mankind, and though he cannot command their obedience, he can assign them their duty."

"What I write is pure nature, and my pen and my soul have ever gone together."

"To fit the powers of thinking and the turn of language to the subject, so as to bring out a clear conclusion that shall hit the point in question and nothing else, is the true criterion of writing."

DOROTHY PARKER
1893–1967

"This novel is not to be tossed lightly aside, but to be hurled with great force."

"The English write much better than we do, and the Irish write better than anybody."

"I can't write five words but that I change seven."

"Why, after all, should readers never be harrowed? Surely there is enough happiness in life without having to go to books for it."

THEODORE PARKER
1810–1882

"I fear we do not know what a power of immediate pleasure and permanent profit is to be had in a good book. The books which help you most are those which make you think the most. The hardest way of learning is by easy reading; every man that tries it finds it so. But a great book that comes from a great thinker,—it is a ship of thought, deep freighted with truth, with beauty too."

BLAISE PASCAL
1623–1662

"The last thing one settles in writing a book is what one should put in first."

"When we see a natural style, we are quite surprised and delighted, for we expected to see an author and we find a man."

BORIS PASTERNAK
1890–1960

"The writer is the Faust of modern society, the only surviving individualist in a mass age. To his orthodox contemporaries he seems a semi-madman."

WALTER PATER
1839–1894

"Books are a refuge, a sort of cloistral refuge, from the vulgarities of the actual world."

"A book, like a person, has its fortunes with one; is lucky or unlucky in the precise moment of its falling in our way, and often by some unhappy accident counts with us for something more than its independent value."

MARK PATTISON
1813–1884

"To a veteran like myself, who have watched the books of forty seasons, there is nothing so old as a new book. An astonishing sameness and want of individuality pervades modern books. The ideas they contain do not seem to have passed through the mind of the writer."

HENRY PEACHAM
1576?–1643?

"Affect not, as some do, that bookish ambition, to be stored with books, and have well-furnished libraries, yet keep their heads empty of knowledge. To desire to have many books, and never to use them, is like a child that will have a candle burning by him all the while he is sleeping."

"Have a care of keeping your books handsome, and well-bound, not casting away overmuch in their gilding or stringing for ostentation sake, like the prayer-books of girls and gallants, which are carried to church but for their outsides."

THOMAS LOVE PEACOCK
1785–1866

"A book that furnishes no quotations is, *me judice,* no book—it is a plaything."

"There is nothing more fit to be looked at than the outside of a book."

EDMUND LESTER PEARSON
1880–1937

"No agreement about books can make us look upon another man with so friendly an eye as the discovery that he belonged to our period, and shared our special enthusiasms about reading, in the years that stretched between the sixth birthday and the sixteenth."

"It is said that a retired English colonel once addressed a letter to one of his friends which ran something like this: 'Dear Jones—I hear you are on the public library board and that you are looking for a new librarian. If this is true I wish you would see if you cannot secure the post for old Higgs, my gardener. He was my orderly for a good many years, but when I came here I brought him along with me. He has puttered about the place for a long time, but really the old fellow is getting too feeble and he ought to have some quiet billet that doesn't need much moving about, where he can end his days in peace. He is an honest old fellow and just the man you are after, I am sure.' "

"For an author to find that a library does not own his most celebrated work is to damn the whole institution in his eyes. What else does the silly place live for?"

WILLIAM PENN
1644–1708

"More true knowledge comes by meditation than by reading; for much reading is an oppression of the mind, and extinguishes the natural candle, which is the reason of so many senseless scholars in the world."

SAMUEL PEPYS
1632–1703

"I know not how to abstain from reading."

"I thank God I can read and never buy a book, though I have a great mind to it."

"Thence homeward by coach and stopped at Martin's, my bookseller, where I saw the French book which I did think to have had for my wife to translate, called *L'escholle des Filles*, but when I came to look in it, it is the most bawdy, lewd book that ever I saw, so that I was ashamed of reading it, and so away home." [January 13, 1668]

"I read through *L'escholle des Filles*, a lewd book, but what do no wrong once to read for information sake. . . . And after I had done it I burned it so that it might not be among my books to my shame, and so at night to supper and to bed." [February 9, 1668]

KATHERINE W. PETERSON
1923–

"The wonderful thing about books is that they allow us to enter imaginatively into someone else's life. And when we do that, we learn to sympathize with other people. But the real surprise is that we also learn truths about ourselves, that somehow we hadn't been able to see before."

"A great novel is a kind of conversion experience. We come away from it changed."

FRANCESCO PETRARCA
1304–1374

"Whether I am being shaved, or having my hair cut, whether I am riding on horseback or taking my meals, I either read myself or get someone to read to me."

"Gold, silver, gems . . . all such things bring only a mute, a superficial pleasure. But books thrill you to the marrow; they talk to you, counsel you, admit you to their living, speaking friendship."

"This book, which would enflame a heart of ice, must set your ardent soul on fire."

"Books have led some to learning and others to madness, when they swallow more than they can digest."

PETRONIUS
D. CA. 66 A.D.

"A man of letters, of the kind that rich men hate."

AUSTIN PHELPS
1820–1890

"Wear the old coat and buy the new book."

WILLIAM LYON PHELPS
1865–1943

"Every one should begin collecting a private library in youth; the instinct of private property, which is fundamental in human beings, can here be cultivated with every advantage and no evils. One should have one's own bookshelves, which should not have doors, glass windows or keys; they should be free and accessible to the hand as well as the eye. The best of mural decorations is books; they are more varied in color and appearance than any wall-paper; they are more attractive in design and they have the prime advantage of being separate personalities, so that if you sit alone in the room in the fire-light you are surrounded with intimate friends."

GEORGE SEARLE PHILLIPS
1816–1882

"Books are our household gods; and we cannot prize them too highly. They are the only gods in all the Mythologies that are ever beautiful and unchangeable; for they betray no man, and love their lovers."

GUILBERT DE PIXERECOURT
1773–1844

"A book is a never-changing friend."

SYLVIA PLATH
1932–1963

"Nothing stinks like a pile of unpublished writing."

"My writing is a hollow and failing substitute for real life, real feeling."

PLATO
427–347 B.C.

"Books are the immortal sons deifying their sires."

PLUTARCH
46–120

"We ought to regard books as we do sweetmeats, not wholly to aim at the pleasantest, but chiefly to respect the wholesomest; not forbidding either, but approving the latter most."

EDGAR ALLAN POE
1809–1849

"The enormous multiplication of books in every branch of knowledge is one of the greatest evils of this age, since it presents one of the most serious obstacles to the acquisition of correct information by throwing in the reader's way piles of lumber in which he must painfully grope for the scraps of useful matter, peradventure interspersed."

"Once upon a midnight dreary, while I pondered weak and
weary,
Over many a quaint and curious volume of forgotten
lore,—"

"Eagerly I wished the morrow;—vainly I had sought to
borrow
From my books surcease of sorrow—sorrow for the lost
Lenore."

"In reading some books we occupy ourselves chiefly with the thoughts of the author; in perusing others, exclusively with our own."

GRAHAM POLLARD
1903–1976

"To attract a collector, a book must appeal to his eye, his mind, or his imagination."

ALEXANDER POPE
1688–1744

"To buy books only because they were published by an eminent printer, is much as if a man should buy clothes that did not fit him, only because made by some famous tailor."

"While pensive poets painful vigils keep
Sleepless themselves they give their readers sleep."

"The bookful blockhead, ignorantly read,
With loads of learned lumber in his head."

"What Authors lose, their Booksellers have won,
So Pimps grow rich, while Gallants are undone."

COLE PORTER
1891–1964

"The girls today in society
Go for classical poetry."

KATHERINE ANNE PORTER
1890–1980

"Most people don't realize that writing is a craft. You have to take your apprenticeship in it like everything else."

"Writing does not exclude the full life; it demands it."

NOAH PORTER, JR.
1811–1892

"No man can read with profit that which he can not learn to read with pleasure."

"In Europe, the essentials of a College or University, are a Library, first of all; then able instructors, and last of all, suitable edifices. In the United States, the prime essentials are thought to be, instructors and college buildings."

"Let me say, then, that the more highly a man is educated, the larger is the library which he needs, that his education may accomplish its highest results."

"It is no figure, and no exaggeration to say, that books are to the scholar, in their quickening influence, what society and conversation are to a man in ordinary life. Books are his best and choicest companions. Without them, and without constant converse with them, he becomes an intellectual hermit. His spirits droop, his vital forces abate, his energies are relaxed, his power to move and waken others departs, and he wastes away by a slow but sure degeneracy."

EMILIE POULSSON
1853–1939

"Books are keys to wisdom's treasure;
Books are gates to lands of pleasure;
Books are paths that upward lead;
Books are friends. Come, let us read."

EZRA POUND
1885–1972

"In depicting 'the motions of the human heart,' the durability of the writing depends upon its exactitude. It is the thing that is true and stays true for the new reader."

> "I had over-prepared the event,
> that much was ominous.
> With middle-ageing care
> I had laid out just the right books.
> I had almost turned down the pages."

"There is no reason why the same man should like the same books at eighteen and forty-eight."

"No man understands a deep book until he has seen and lived at least part of its contents."

"The secret of popular writing is never to put more on a given page than the common reader can lap off it with no strain whatsoever on his habitually slack attention."

LAWRENCE CLARK POWELL
1906–

"What are some deficiencies in academic librarians?

The first is to me the greatest: too few librarians suffer from the disease Dibdin called bibliomania. We are paradoxically not a bookish profession. 'Too busy to read' is our excuse, and it is a tragic one. To be sure, we do not need more dilettantes who 'just love' books. Love is not enough. Give us librarians who have an overwhelming passion for books, who are bookmen by birth and by choice, by education, profession, and hobby. Properly channeled and directed, this passion for books is the greatest single basic asset a librarian can have."

"There is no moderate life for a bookman. Suspect is he who lives a bookish life from eight to five, then shuts the door on heaven-on-earth, and turns to cards or golf or worse. Give me the man whose life is encircled by books, who lives and plays, wakes and dreams, sells or lends, and everlastingly reads books, who practices what he preaches, the true gospel that, next to mother's milk, books are the best food. Thus I view with alarm the invasion of the book world by barbarians who neither believe in books for their totality of being, their fusion of form and content, nor have any sentimental feelings toward the book as a thing-in-itself."

"There is no way of communicating with people who, by an imbalance of thinking over feeling, do not respond to the wedding of form and content which makes Milton in seventeenth-century calf or sheep infinitely more powerful than the great Puritan in Fabrikoid or on film. As if to say that Helen of Troy could have launched those ships or burned those towers by remote control, rather than by the presence of her face and form, by the soft words, the ringing words her sweet lips said."

"I believe that books—those beautiful blends of form and spirit—have a future fully as glorious as their past; that to disbelieve this is an act of faithlessness, is dangerous, and could lead to the downfall of the kind of librarianship in which the book is central and basic. I know that I am not alone in my belief, my faith, my love, and I call on booklovers everywhere to close ranks, face the invaders, and give them the works, preferably in elephant folio."

"I have heard people confess that once they started a book they felt obliged perhaps out of courtesy to the author to finish it. Not I. If the book by its style does not compel me to read it, I return it to the shelf and look henceforth with suspicion on its author. There is no time for bad books, dull books."

JOHN COOPER POWYS
1872–1963

"Books are man's rational protest against the irrational, man's pitiful protest against the implacable, man's ideal against the world's real, man's word against the cosmic dumbness, man's life against the planetary death, man's revelations of the God within him, man's repartee to the God without him. Whoever touches a book touches not only 'a man' but Man. Man is the animal who weeps and laughs—and writes. If the first Prometheus brought fire from heaven in a fennel-stalk, the last will take it back—in a book."

MATTHEW PRIOR
1664–1721

"For some in ancient books delight;
Others prefer what moderns write:
Now I should be extremely loth
Not to be thought expert in both."

"Let him be kept from paper, pen, and ink;
So may he cease to write, and learn to think."

" 'Tis not how well an author says,
But 'tis how much, that gathers praise."

ADELAIDE ANN PROCTER
1825–1864

"My books lie closed upon the shelf;
I miss the old heart in myself."

MARCEL PROUST
1871–1922

"Our journalism forces us to take an interest in some fresh triviality every day, whereas only three or four books in a lifetime give us anything that is of importance."

"They buried him, but all through the night of mourning, in the lighted windows, his books arranged three by three kept watch like angels with outspread wings and seemed, for him who was no more, the symbol of his resurrection."

"Our passions shape our books, repose writes them in the intervals."

MARIO PUZO
1920–

"Never let a domestic quarrel ruin a day's writing. If you can't start the next day fresh, get rid of your wife."

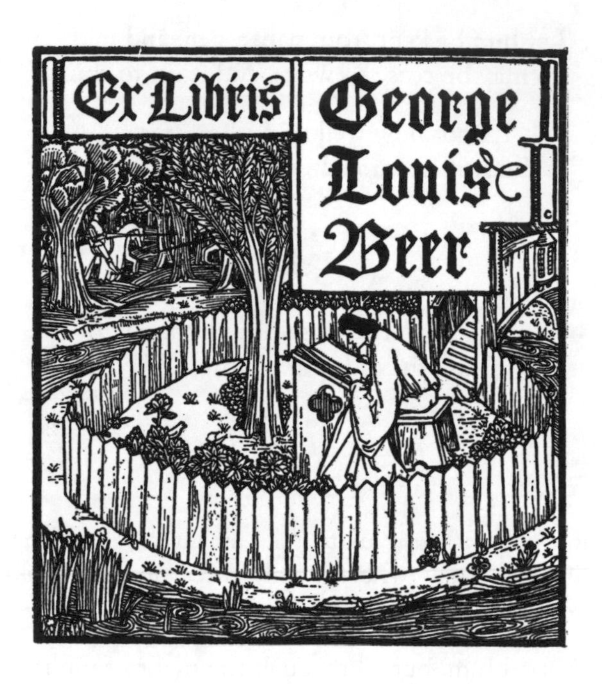
Ex Libris
George
Louis
Beer

FRANCIS QUARLES
1592–1644

"I wish thee as much pleasure in the reading, as I had in the writing."

QUINTILIAN
42–115

"Reading is free, and does not exhaust itself with the act, but may be repeated, in case you are in doubt, or wish to impress it deeply on the memory. Let us repeat it; and—just as we swallow our food masticated and nearly fluid, in order that it may be more easily digested—so our reading should not be delivered to the memory in its crude state, but sweetened and worked up by frequent repetition."

"Every good writer is to be read, and diligently; and, when the volume is finished, is to be gone through again from the beginning."

"Let our literary compositions be laid aside for some time, that we may after a reasonable period return to their perusal, and find them, as it were, altogether new to us."

LEROY
The BOOK-WORM
Carl S. Junge
GOBLE

JEAN-JOSEPH RABÉARIVELO
1901–1937

"One day some young poet
Will make your impossible wish come true
By knowing your books,
Books as rare as flowers underground,
Written for a hundred friends."

"The books you write
Will wrestle with what's unreal,
Unreal from being too real
Like dreams."

FRANÇOIS RABELAIS
1494?–1553

"It becomes you to be wise, to smell, feel and have in estimation, these fair, godly books, stuffed with high conceptions."

WALTER RALEIGH
1861–1922

"No one who understands the real thing cares twopence about the dull student, except as a man and a brother. Drink with him, pray with him; don't read with him."

"There is no time so good to read a book as when you have just bought it and brought it home."

DAVID A. RANDALL
1905–1975

"In my ten years of academic associations I have found very few graduates of library school who were competent rare bookmen or who could pull their weight with a good bookstore clerk.... What it all adds up to is that a proper appreciation of the value of this type of books is an emotional and not an intellectual process, like love. And that can't be taught in schools."

BURTON RASCOE
1892–1957

"What no wife of a writer can understand is that a writer is working when he is staring out of the window."

ERNEST RENAN
1823–1892

"The talent of historians lies in their creating a true ensemble out of facts which are but half-true."

JULES RENARD
1864–1910

"Thank God, Achilles and Don Quixote are well enough known so that we can dispense with reading Homer and Cervantes."

"In literature, there are only oxen. The biggest ones are the geniuses—the ones who toil eighteen hours a day without tiring."

"Talent is a question of quantity. Talent does not write one page: it writes three hundred."

"The profession of letters is, after all, the only one in which one can make no money without being ridiculous."

KENNETH REXROTH
1905–1982

"I've had it with these cheap sons of bitches who claim they love poetry but never buy a book."

BALTHASAR BONIFACIUS RHODIGINUS
1584–1659

"But how can I live here without my books? I really seem to myself crippled and only half myself; for if, as the great Orator used to say, arms are a soldier's members, surely books are the limbs of a scholar. Corasius says: Of a truth, he who would deprive me of books, my old friends, would take away all the delight of my life, nay, I will even say all desire of living."

JEAN RHYS
1890–1979

"If I stop writing my life will have been an abject failure. It is that already to other people. But it could be an abject failure to myself. I will not have earned death."

"All of a writer that matters is in the book or books. It is idiotic to be curious about the person."

ETHEL F. RICHARDSON
1870–1946

"There are enough women to do the childbearing and childrearing. I know of none who can write my books."

SAMUEL RICHARDSON
1689–1761

"We have great opportunities at the university of knowing human nature from books, the calm result of the wise men's wisdom."

ARMAND JEAN DU PLESSIS, DUC DE RICHELIEU
1585–1642

"If you give me six lines written by the hand of the most honest of men, I will find something in them which will hang him."

MORDECAI RICHLER
1931–

"If you caricature friends in your first novel they will be upset, but if you don't they will feel betrayed."

JAMES RIDLEY
1736–1765

"It is necessary that authors should be poor; first, because overeating spoils wit and conceit; and secondly, because none but poor dogs will ever be at the pains of writing at such a rate."

"To brand a book with infamy is to insure its sale."

RAINER MARIA RILKE
1875–1926

"Find out the reason that commands you to write; see whether it has spread its roots into the very depth of your heart; confess to yourself you would have to die if you were forbidden to write."

"I never read anything concerning my work. I feel that criticism is a letter to the public which the author, since it is not directed to him, does not have to open and read."

JOAN RIVERS
1937–

"If you're good-looking, that's enough. No man ever put his hand up a dress looking for a library card."

WILLIAM ROBERTS
1682–1940

"The companionship of books is unquestionably one of the greatest antidotes to the ravages of time, and study is better than all medical formulas for the prolongation of life."

PAUL ROBESON
1898–1976

"So for me in high school there would be four years of Latin and then in college four more years of Latin and Greek. Closely my father watched my studies, and was with me page by page through Virgil and Homer and the other classics in which he was well grounded."

SAMUEL ROGERS
1763–1855

"During my whole life I have borne in mind the speech of a woman to Philip of Macedon: 'I appeal from Philip drunk to Philip sober.' After writing anything in the excitement of the moment, and being greatly pleased with it, I have always put it by for a day or two; and then carefully considering it in every possible light, I have altered it to the best of my judgment; thus appealing from myself drunk to myself sober."

"I lived to write, and wrote to live."

WILL ROGERS
1879–1935

"I never was much on this book reading, for it takes 'em too long to describe the color of the eyes of all the characters."

"When you put down the good things you ought to have done, and leave out the bad ones you did do—well, that's Memoirs."

"There ain't nothing that breaks up homes, country, and nations like somebody publishing their memoirs."

CARL PURINGTON ROLLINS
1880–1960

"I would hardly go so far as to say that a book without an autograph, a bookplate, a thumb mark, a marginal note, a dog-ear, a slightly (but only slightly, please!) broken back, is but half a book. Yet there is something to be said for the notion that a book fresh from the press or the publisher's shelf is like a feast uneaten, a wine untasted, a colt unbroken, a talent unused. Such a book is too virginal for any but a furtive and frigid bibliotaph. For me, I prefer 'good, second-hand condition'—withpreferably a few stains of varied sorts, and a scribbled comment or two by a learned or ribald owner. Such a book has at some time found a friend and been welcomed to someone's hearth."

ELEANOR ROOSEVELT
1884–1962

"The reason that fiction is more interesting than any other form of literature to those of us who really like to study people, is that in fiction the author can really tell the truth without hurting anyone and without humiliating himself too much."

FRANKLIN D. ROOSEVELT
1882–1945

"We all know that books burn, yet we have the greater knowledge that books cannot be killed by fire. People die, but books never die."

AMANDA MCKITTRICK ROS
1861–1939

"I don't believe in publishers. . . . I consider they're too grabby altogether. They love to keep the Sabbath and everything else they can lay their hands on."

A. S. W. ROSENBACH
1876–1952

"After love, book collecting is the most exhilarating sport of all."

"I have seen men hazard their fortunes, go on long journeys halfway around the world, forge friendships, even lie, cheat and steal, all for the gain of a book."

"Attending book auctions is for the booklover the greatest, the most stirring of adventures. The lust of books is here seen at its heights: faces that are usually poker portraits become sharply distorted, eyes which ordinarily indulge an almost studied innocence shoot sudden darts of fire."

"Book collectors, I make no exceptions, are buzzards who stretch their wings in anticipation as they wait patiently for a colleague's demise; and then they swoop down and ghoulishly grab some long-coveted treasure from the dear departed's trove."

"I suppose there are people—I've been told there are intelligent people—who would just as soon have an edition of Keats's *Poems*, for example, well printed on good paper, in a handsome modern binding, as a first edition in its original boards! I hope I never meet them."

"Of all the branches of the sport connected with book collecting, that of attending book auctions is the greatest, the most stirring. I presume some patient mathematician knows the number of facets of the Koh-i-nur diamond, but no one will ever be able to count the emotional reflections which take place during a book auction in the hearts and minds of men and women who are enamored of books. The book auction is an adventure. Other adventures may lose their glamour if you repeat them, but each experience at a sale of books brings a delightful thrill never to be duplicated."

"Uncle Moses quickly came down from his ladder and gloated proudly over the newly arrived pile of books. Then he fairly beamed as he turned to me.

'My boy,' he exclaimed, 'Americana! That's the stuff to collect!' "

ALICE ROSSI
1922–

"Abridgment of any published book or essay is an assault, a cutting or pruning by one mind of the work of another."

LEO ROSTEN
1908–

"I have always loved the idea of those pious Jews who envisaged the world to come: as an immense library, where all the truly good books written by man would be available to the righteous dead."

JEAN JACQUES ROUSSEAU
1712–1778

"Too much reading hinders knowledge. We think we know what we have read, and consider ourselves excused from learning it."

"I hate books, for they only teach people to talk about what they do not understand."

"People have wanted to make novel-reading useful to the young; I can't think of anything more senseless: it's like setting fire to the house so that the fire-brigade can be called out."

JOSEPH ROUX
1834–1905

"Two sort of writers possess genius; those who think and those who cause others to think."

JOHN RUSKIN
1819–1900

"To use books rightly, is to go to them for help; to appeal to them when our knowledge and power fail; to be led by them into wider sight and purer concentration than our own, and to receive from them the united sentence of the judges and councils of all time, against our solitary and unstable opinions."

"For all books are divisible into two classes, the books of the hour, and the books of all time. Make this distinction—it is not one of quality only. It is not merely the bad book that does not last, and the good one that does. There are good books for the hour, and bad ones for all time."

"If a book is worth reading, it is worth buying."

"We call ourselves a rich nation, and we are filthy and foolish enough to thumb each other's books out of circulating libraries!"

"What do we, as a nation, care about books? How much do you think we spend altogether on our libraries, public or private, as compared with what we spend on our horses?"

"Each book that a young girl touches should be bound in white vellum."

"How long most people would look at the best book before they would give the price of a large turbot for it!"

"Life being short and the quiet hours of it few, we ought to waste none of them in reading valueless books."

"Keep the modern magazine and novel out of your girl's way; turn her loose into the old library every wet day, and let her alone."

"At least be sure that you go to the author to get at *his* meaning, not to find yours."

BERTRAND RUSSELL
1872–1970

"I have a certain hesitation in starting my biography too soon for fear of something important having not yet happened. Suppose I should end my days as President of Mexico; the biography would seem incomplete if it did not mention this fact."

"A man without a bias cannot write interesting history—if indeed such a man exists."

JOHN RUSSELL
1919–

"I cannot think of a great blessing than to die in one's own bed, without warning or discomfort, on the last page of the new book that we most wanted to read."

Ex Libris
Stanley Shepard

VITA SACKVILLE-WEST
1892–1962

"It is never wise to disregard the sagacity of those who do not learn their lore from books."

MICHAEL SADLEIR
1888–1957

"In nature, the bird who gets up earliest catches the most worms; but in book-collecting, the prizes fall to birds who know worms when they see them."

FRANÇOISE SAGAN
1935–

"Of course the illusion of art is to make one believe that great literature is very close to life, but exactly the opposite is true. Life is amorphous, literature is formal."

"I shall live badly if I do not write, and I shall write badly if I do not live."

"Writing is just having a sheet of paper, a pen and not a shadow of an idea of what you're going to say."

CHARLES AUGUSTIN SAINT-BEUVE
1809–1869

"Nothing is more painful to me than the disdain with which people treat second-rate authors, as if there were room only for the first-raters."

J. D. SALINGER
1919–

"I'm quite illiterate, but I read a lot."

GEORGE SAND
1804–1876

"The reader turns away from a book where all the characters are good without shades or weakness; he knows very well that this isn't human."

CARL SANDBURG
1878–1967

"The peace of great books be for you,
Stains of pressed clover leaves on pages,
Bleach of the light of years held in leather."

GEORGE SANTAYANA
1863–1952

"[Emerson] read transcendentally, not historically, to learn what he himself felt, not what others might have felt before him. And to feed on books, for a philosopher or a poet, is still to starve. Books can help him to acquire form, or to avoid pitfalls; they cannot supply him with substance, if he is to have any."

"Near a window overlooking the garden of Exeter he found his pile of books, safe and complete on the long oaken reading-desk. His name on a slip of paper, stuck in the top book, sufficed to reserve them all. That alcove, like a cell in a beehive, where you worked silently and alone, but under the eye of community and in its service; that glimpse of a cloistered garden; that roof with its wooden skeleton exposed to view, and become a picturesque decoration; that musty smell of the old books, bound in calf, which he was reading—all this intimately transported him into a bygone age, into a world of pathos and duty, of love and war. Where was it fled, that enchantment, that courage, that merriment, that splendour?"

WILLIAM SAROYAN
1908–1981

"When the two boys entered the public library, they entered an area of profound and solemn silence, as if the funeral services were still going on. There were old men reading newspapers. There were town philosophers sitting over enormous books. There were high school boys and girls doing research, but everyone was hushed, because they were seeking wisdom. They were in the presence of books. They were trying to find out."

"The two friends moved off into still greater realms of mystery and adventure. Lionel pointed out more books to Ulysses. 'These,' he said. 'And those over there. And these. All books, Ulysses.' He stopped a moment to think. 'I wonder what they say in all these books.' He pointed out a whole vast area of them, five shelves full of them. 'All these,' he said—'I wonder what they say.' "

MAY SARTON
1912–1995

"Anyone who is going to be a writer knows enough at fifteen to write several novels."

JOHN GODFREY SAXE
1816–1887

"I love vast libraries; yet there is a doubt
If one be better with them or without,—
Unless he uses them wisely, and indeed,
Knows the high art of what and how to read,
At learning's fountain it is sweet to drink,
But 't is a nobler privilege to think."

DOROTHY L. SAYERS
1893–1957

"Books . . . are like lobster shells, we surround ourselves with 'em, then we grow out of 'em and leave 'em behind, as evidence of our earlier stage of development."

FRIEDRICH VON SCHLEGEL
1772–1829

"A historian is a prophet in reverse."

ARTHUR A. SCHOMBURG
1874–1938

"All these books are like meat without salt, they bear no analogy to our own, it would be a wise plan for us to lay down a course of study in Negro History and achievements."

"Many histories of our people in slavery, peace, and war are written and each serves a purpose. These books have disseminated the fragmentary knowledge where the spark of learning has awakened the soul to thirst for more and better food."

ARTHUR SCHOPENHAUER
1788–1860

"To buy books would be a good thing if we also could buy the time to read them. As it is, the act of purchasing them is often mistaken for the assimilation and mastering of their content."

"To put away one's original thoughts in order to take up a book is the sin against the Holy Ghost."

"Any good book that is at all important ought to be at once read through twice."

"To expect a man to retain everything that he has ever read is like expecting him to carry about in his body everything that he has ever eaten."

M. LINCOLN SCHUSTER
1897–1970

"You ask for the distinction between the terms 'Editor' and 'Publisher': an editor selects manuscripts; a publisher selects editors."

WALTER SCOTT
1771–1832

"Please return this book; I find that though many of my friends are poor arithmeticians, they are nearly all good book-keepers."

"And better had they ne'er been born,
Who read to doubt, or read to scorn."

"Muddling among old books has the quality of a sedative, and saves the wear and tear of an overwrought brain."

"But no one shall find me rowing against the stream. I care not who knows it—I write for the general amusement."

"Waverley drove through the sea of books, like a vessel without a pilot or a rudder."

ARMAND LOUIS MAURICE SEGUIER
1770–1831

"If someone wishes to seduce me, he has only to offer me books."

JOHN SELDEN
1584–1654

"In quoting of books, quote such authors as are usually read; others you may read for your own satisfaction, but not name them."

LUCIUS ANNAEUS SENECA
4 B.C.–65 A.D.

"No book can be so good as to be profitable when negligently read."

"A large library is apt to distract rather than to instruct the learner; it is much better to be confined to a few authors than to wander at random over many."

"It matters not how many books you have—but how good those are which you do possess."

"You must linger among a limited number of master-thinkers, and digest their works, if you would derive ideas which shall win firm hold in your mind."

MARQUISE MARIE DE SÉVIGNÉ
1626–1696

"Bad books are better than no books at all."

FIRST EARL OF SHAFTESBURY
1621–1683

"Of all artificial relations formed between mankind, the most capricious and variable is that of author and reader."

WILLIAM SHAKESPEARE
1564–1616

"Knowing I loved my books, he furnished me,
From mine own library, with volumes that
I prize above my dukedom."

"Me, poor man, my library
Was dukedom large enough."

"Sir, he hath never fed of the dainties that are bred in a book. He hath not eat paper, as it were; he hath not drunk ink: his intellect is not replenished; he is only an animal, only sensible in the duller parts."

"Was ever book containing such vile matter
So fairly bound? O, that deceit should dwell
In such a gorgeous palace!"

"To be a well-favoured man is a gift of fortune; but to write and read comes by nature."

"Come, and take choice of all my library;
And so beguile thy sorrow."

"[Polonius] What do you read, my lord?
[Hamlet] Words, words, words."

"Assist me some extemporal god of rime, for I am sure I shall turn sonneteer. Devise, wit; write, pen; for I am for whole volumes in folio."

"Thou has most traitorously corrupted the youth of the realm in erecting a grammar school; and whereas, before, our forefathers had no other books but the score and the tally, thou hast caused printing to be used; and, contrary to the king, his crown and dignity, thou hast built a paper-mill."

"We turned o'er many books together."

"Yet if my name were liable to fear,
I do not know the man I should avoid
So soon as that spare Cassius. He reads much."

"Study is like the heaven's glorious sun,
That will not be deep-search'd with saucy looks,
Small have continual plodders ever won,
Save base authority from others' books."

"O let my books be then the eloquence
And dumb presagers of my speaking breast;
Who plead for love, and look for recompense,
More than that tongue that more than hath express'd.
O learn to read what silent love hath writ:
To hear with eyes belong to love's fine writ."

"The books, the arts, the academes,
That show, contain, and nourish all the world."

"Remember
First to possess his books; for without them
He's but a sot, as I am."

"I see, lady, the gentleman is not in your books."

"Study is like the heaven's glorious sun,
That will not be deep-search'd with saucy looks;
Small have continual plodders ever won,
Save base authority from others' books."

"From women's eyes this doctrine I derive;
They are the ground, the books, the academes,
From whence doth spring the true Promethean fire."

WILLIAM SHARP
1856–1905

"Mark me, what dust there is! But should there dart
Along these rows the Bookman's eager eyes
Lit with a first-edition-glow surmise—
Then shalt thou see me ope, and turn apart
These frail glazed doors, and rend thy inmost heart
With many a rare unpurchasable prize."

GEORGE BERNARD SHAW
1856–1950

"Only in books has mankind known perfect truth, love and beauty."

"Not until an author has become so familiar that we are quite at our ease with him, and are up to his tricks of manner, do we cease to imagine that he is, relatively to older writers, terribly serious."

"Of the millions of books in the world, there are very few that make any permanent mark on the minds of those who read them."

"The contrast between the wisdom of our literature and the folly of our rulers and voters is a melancholy proof that people get nothing out of books except what they bring to them, and that even when the books explode their prejudices and rebuke their villainies they will read their own dispositions into the books in spite of the authors, and hang up their instruments of torture and their bullet-riddled banners in the very temples of Mercy and Peace."

"With the world's bookshelves loaded with fascinating and inspired books, the very manna sent down from heaven to feed your souls, you are forced to read a hideous imposture called a school book, written by a man who cannot write: a book from which no human being can learn anything: a book which, though you may decipher it, you cannot in any fruitful sense read, though the enforced attempt will make you loathe the sight of a book all the rest of your life."

". . . a book is like a child: it is easier to bring it into the world than to control it when it is launched there. As long as I kept sending my novels to the publishers, they were as safe from publicity as they would have been in the fire, where I had better, perhaps, have put them. But when I flung them aside as failures they almost instantly began to shew signs of life."

"Once, when I was a guest in a Manchester club, I was insulted by one of the members so offensively that I had to lecture him severely on his breach of club manners, and warn him that my host might complain to the Committee. What annoyed him was not my uncompromising refusal to accept

Jehovah as a god, but that I had denied the omniscience and infallibility of Shakespear[sic]."

"[Swindon]: 'I cant believe it! What will History say?' [Burgoyne]: 'History, sir, will tell lies, as usual.' "

"Reading made Don Quixote a gentleman. Believing what he read made him mad."

"Novelists are not normal human citizens."

"For nearly twenty years I have been a published author. . . . But I have never yet seen a book of mine offered for sale in a shop window."

"Keep away from books; and from men who get their ideas from books, and your own books will always be fresh."

"Well-printed books are just as scarce as well-written ones, and every author should remember that the most costly books derive their value from the craft of the printer and not from the author's genius."

"With the single exception of Homer, there is no eminent writer, not even Sir Walter Scott, whom I can despise so entirely as I despise Shakespeare, when I measure my mind against his. . . . It would positively be a relief to me to dig him up and throw stones at him."

"You must not suppose, because I am a man of letters, that I never tried to earn an honest living."

JOHN SHEFFIELD, DUKE OF BUCKINGHAM
1648–1721

"Of all those arts in which the wise excel,
Nature's chief masterpiece is writing well."

PERCY BYSSHE SHELLEY
1792–1822

"Poets are the trumpets that sing to battle; poets are the unacknowledged legislators of the world."

RICHARD BRINSLEY SHERIDAN
1751–1816

"You write with ease, to show your breeding,
But easy writing's vile hard reading."

"Madam, a circulating library in a town is as an evergreen tree of diabolical knowledge!"

"You shall see them on a beautiful quarto page, where a neat rivulet of text shall meander through a meadow of margin."

THOMAS SHERIDAN
1687–1738

"While you converse with lords and dukes,
I have their betters here—my books,
Fixed in an elbow-chair at ease,
I choose companions as I please."

MARY MARTHA SHERWOOD
1775–1851

" 'And why not?' returned the fakeer, 'I can read books and men too, and I tell you that the latter is a much more profitable branch of study than the former.' "

LEE SHIPPEY
1884–1969

"The right book at the right time may mean more in a person's life than anything else."

JAMES SHIRLEY
1596–1666

"There's a lady for my humour!
A pretty book of flesh and blood, and well
Bound up, in a fair letter, too. Would I
Had her, with all the Errata."

NEVIL SHUTE
1899–1960

"In my opinion the readers of novels are far more intelligent than unsuccessful authors will believe."

GEORGES SIMENON
1903–1989

"Writing is not a profession but a vocation of unhappiness."

"For me, Literature with a capital L is rubbish."

"I write fast, because I have not the brains to write slow."

WILLIAM GILMORE SIMMS
1806–1870

"The novelist cannot do always as he would with his own creations."

PAUL SIMON
1941–

"I am a rock; I am an island.
I have my books and my poetry to protect me."

ISAAC BASHEVIS SINGER
1904–1991

"God is a writer and we are both the heroes and the readers."

"Experience has shown me that there are no miracles in writing. The only thing that produces good writing is hard work. It's impossible to write a good story by carrying a rabbit's foot in your pocket."

" 'Why don't you sell books here? There are so many people here.'

'You mean Coney Island? Here they come to eat popcorn, not to read books.' "

EDITH SITWELL
1887–1964

"Poetry ennobles the heart and the eyes, and unveils the meaning of all things upon which the heart and the eyes dwell. It discovers the secret rays of the universe, and restores to us forgotten paradise."

WILLIAM SHENSTONE
1714–1763

"His knowledge of books had in some degree diminished his knowledge of the world."

SAMUEL SMILES
1812–1904

"The great and good do not die even in this world. Embalmed in books, their spirits walk abroad. The book is a living voice. It is an intellect to which one listens."

ALEXANDER SMITH
1830–1867

"I go into my library and all history rolls before me. I breathe the morning air of the world while the scent of Eden's roses yet linger in it. . . . I see the pyramids of Alexander. . . . I sit as in a theatre—the stage is time, the play is the play of the world."

"[Books are] the true Elysian fields where the spirits of the dead converse, and into these fields a mortal may venture unappalled."

"Books are a finer world within the world. . . . When I go to my long sleep, on a book will my head be pillowed."

LOGAN PEARSALL SMITH
1865–1946

"This nice and subtle happiness of reading, this joy not chilled by age, this polite and unpunished vice, this selfish, serene life-long intoxication."

"People say that life is the thing, but I prefer reading."

"There are readers—and I am one of them—whose reading is rather like a series of intoxications. We fall in love with a book; it is our book, we feel, for life; we shall not need another. We cram-throat our friends with it in the cruellest fashion; make it a Gospel, which we preach in a spirit of propaganda and indignation, putting a woe on the world for a neglect of which last week we were equally guilty."

"Every author, however modest, keeps a most outrageous vanity chained like a madman in the padded cell of his breast."

"A best seller is the gilded tomb of a mediocre talent."

RED SMITH
1905–1982

"There's nothing to writing. All you do is sit down at the typewriter and open a vein."

SYDNEY SMITH
1771–1845

"No furniture is so charming as books. . . . Even if you never open them, or read a single word; the plainest row of cloth or paper covered books is more significant of refinement than the most elaborately carved etagere or sideboard."

"I never read a book before reviewing it, it prejudices a man so."

"Some men have only one book in them; others, a library."

SOCRATES
469–399 B.C.

"Employ your time in improving yourself by other men's writings so that you shall come easily by what others have labored hard for."

ALEKSANDER SOLZHENITSYN
1918–

"A great writer is, so to speak, a second government in his country. And for that reason, no regime has ever loved great writers, only minor ones."

SUSAN SONTAG
1933–

"The writer is either a practicing recluse or a delinquent, guilt-ridden one; or both. Usually both."

"Perversity is the muse of modern literature."

ROBERT SOUTHEY
1774–1843

"Coleridge is gone to Devonshire, and I was going to say I am alone, but the sight of Shakespeare, and Spenser, Milton, and the Bible, on my table, and Castanheda, and Barros, and Osorio at my elbow, tell me I am in the best of all possible company."

"Literary fame is the only fame of which a wise man ought to be ambitious, because it is the only lasting and living fame."

"Literature cannot be the business of a woman's life, and it ought not to be."

"I am frankly a little mad about books."

E. MILLICENT SOWERBY
1883–1977

"Rare-book people have this in common with poets: they too are born, not made."

"The time necessarily spent in the Cambridge University Library had convinced me that a library was no place in which to work should one be interested in books. For anyone with a flair for making catalogue cards, it might be an ideal place in which to fulfill one's ambition, but a flair for books is an entirely different matter."

HERBERT SPENCER
1820–1903

"Reading is seeing by proxy."

MARION H. SPIELMANN
1858–1948

"Of course, I admire the Morris volumes—but, according to my definition, they are really not books at all. A book is primarily intended to be read, and any features in illustration or decoration, in ornament, page, or paper arrangement, that obviously conspire against the reading of the book, or the concentration of the reader, are wrong in art and indefensible in practice."

JOHN COLLINGS SQUIRE
1884–1958

"Let sleep go. Let the morrow's duties go. Let health, prudence, and honour go. The bedside book for me is the book that will longest keep me awake."

LELAND STANFORD
1824–1893

"Read some every day. Always have at least one good book lying on your table. Read carefully, endeavor to understand and remember what you read. . . . You will often find your mind wandering from the page to other subjects. By reading it over again you inflict a sort of punishment on your mind which it will be sure to heed finally."

HENRY M. STANLEY
1841–1904

"You ask me what books I carried with me to take across Africa. I carried a great many—three loads, or about 180 lbs. weight; but as my men lessened in numbers stricken by famine, fighting, and sickness, they were one by one reluctantly thrown away, until finally, when less than 300 miles from the Atlantic, I possessed only the Bible, Shakespeare, Carlyle's *Sartor Resartus*, Norie's *Navigation*, and *Nautical Almanac* for 1877."

VINCENT STARRETT
1886–1974

"When we are collecting books, we are collecting happiness."

"And let me say at once that I have had more genuine happiness collecting books than in any other single transaction in life. I have always been more interested in other men's books than in my own; if it had been otherwise, I might conceivably have done more and better creative work of my own."

"There is only one reason for selling one's books, and that is poverty; there is no other justification."

"When Lowell, during what proved to be his final illness, was asked by somebody how he was, he looked up from the book he had been reading and answered: 'I don't know and I don't care. I'm reading *Rob Roy.*' "

"To the incurable booklover books are the beginning and the end of life; indeed, they are its meaning, the answer to its riddle. For him, mankind, like ancient Gaul, is divided into three parts: those who write books, those who read them and an innumerable company who exist or have existed merely to be written about."

"There is a superstition in the book trade that all books about Lincoln sell, that all books about dogs sell, and that all books by and about doctors sell. Ergo, say the publishers and booksellers, the crafty inkster who can combine these favorite subjects, and produce a book about Lincoln's doctor's dog, is going to clean up."

"I was born in a bookshop or so close to it as to be able to claim the distinction. It was in a bookshop that I first learned the odor of books, first read the immortal works of George Alfred Henty, and felt the first vague stirrings of envy, admiration and authorship. If I were not a writer of books, I would be a bookseller, selling the dreams and solutions of other writers across the counter. Preferably, I think, an antiquarian bookseller. Books to me are the most important things in life after food, water, dogs, cats, girls, and the usual catalogue of imperatives."

"Superficially it may appear that I am more interested in books than in people; but I think it nearer the mark to say that I am more interested in people as they are revealed to me in books than as they reveal themselves to me in daily contact."

RICHARD STEELE
1672–1729

"Reading is to the mind what exercise is to the body."

WALLACE STEGNER
1909–1993

"When I was twenty I was in love with words, a wordsmith. I didn't know enough to know when people were letting words get in their way. Now I like the words to disappear, like a transparent curtain."

GERTRUDE STEIN
1874–1946

"I write for myself and strangers. The strangers, dear Readers, are an afterthought."

"Besides Shakespeare and me, who do you think there is?"

JOHN STEINBECK
1902–1968

"The profession of book writing makes horse racing seem like a solid, stable business."

"Hard-covered books break up friendships. You loan a hard-covered book to a friend and when he doesn't return it you get mad at him. It makes you mean and petty. But twenty-five-cent books are different."

GLORIA STEINEM
1934–

"Writing is the only thing that . . . when I'm doing it, I don't feel that I should be doing something else instead."

STENDAHL
1783–1842

"To do my duty as a traveler I presented myself at Monsieur Bodoni's, the celebrated printer. I was agreeably surprised. This Piedmontais is not at all ostentatious, but is in love with his art. After having shown me all his French authors he demanded of me which I preferred, the *Telemaque* of Fenelon, the Racine, or the Boileau. I vowed all these seemed equally beautiful. 'Ah, Monsieur,' cried Bodoni, 'you don't see the title of the Boileau!' I looked at it for a long time, and was forced to admit that I could not see anything more perfect in that title than in the others. 'Ah, Monsieur,' again expostulated Bodoni, '*Boileau Despreaux* in one single line of capitals!

I spent six months before I could decide upon exactly that type.' "

"A novel is a mirror walking along a main road."

LESLIE STEPHEN
1832–1904

"To read a book in the true sense, to read it, that is, not as a critic but in the spirit of enjoyment—is to lay aside for the moment one's own personality and to become a part of the author."

STEWART STERN
1922–

" 'You know something? You read too many comic books.' "

LAURENCE STERNE
1713–1768

"Digressions, incontestably, are the sunshine;—they are the life, the soul of reading;—take them out of this book for instance,—you might as well take the book along with them."

"The life of a writer is not so much a state of composition, as a state of warfare."

HENRY STEVENS, JR.
1819–1886

"The manufacture of a beautiful and durable book costs little if anything more, it is believed, than it does to manufacture a clumsy and unsightly one. Good taste, skill and severe training are as requisite and necessary in the proper production of books as in any other of the fine arts. The well recognized 'lines of beauty' are as essential and well defined in the one case as in the other."

WALLACE STEVENS
1879–1955

"Life is the reflection of literature."

"Authors are actors, books are theatres."

ROBERT LOUIS STEVENSON
1850–1894

"Biography . . . performs for us some of the work of fiction, reminding us, that is, of the truly mangled tissue of man's nature and how huge faults and virtues cohabit and persevere in the same character."

"Books are good enough in their own way, but they are a mighty bloodless substitute for life."

"There is no quite good book without a good morality; but the world is wide, and so are morals."

"To pass from hearing great literature to reading it is to take a great and dangerous step."

"Fiction is to the grown man what play is to the child; it is there that he changes the atmosphere and tenor of his life."

COLTON STORM
1908–1988

"The American collector is a wondrous and fearsome beast. The valiant librarian, in his shining armor, is often sorely beset with doubts about rare book collectors, because normally he knows so few of them. Is he meeting a fire-eating guardian of treasure, or a somewhat reluctant dragon? Only a visit to the dragon's lair will unravel the mystery."

REX STOUT
1886–1975

"My theory is that people who don't like detective stories are anarchists."

HARRIET BEECHER STOWE
1811–1896

"Works of fiction, if only well gotten up, have always their advantages in the hearts of listeners over plain, homely truth."

"If I am to write I must have a room to myself that will be my room."

"I feel now that the time is come when even a woman . . . who can speak a word for freedom and humanity is bound to speak. I hope that every woman who can write will not be silent."

LYTTON STRACHEY
1880–1932

"To preserve a becoming brevity, a brevity which excludes everything that is redundant and nothing that is significant, that surely is the first duty of the biographer."

NORMAN H. STROUSE
1906–1993

"I am always mindful, in thinking of books, that we, as men & women, are creatures of endless curiosity, speculating always on the multiple facets of our compositions and our history and our world, and that only books can satisfy that boundless desire to know. Books certainly are the greatest treasures we have; in them are contained all religions and all amusements, all passions and occupations, all that we know on earth and what we suspect of heaven."

WILLIAM STYRON
1925–

"Reading—the best state yet to keep absolute loneliness at bay."

"A great book should leave you with many experiences, and slightly exhausted at the end. You live several lives while reading it."

"The good writing of any age has always been the product of someone's neurosis, and we'd have a mighty dull literature if all the writers that came along were a bunch of happy chuckleheads."

JONATHAN SWIFT
1667–1745

"The most accomplished way of using books at present is twofold; either, first, to serve them as men do lords, learn their titles exactly and then brag of their acquaintance. Or, secondly, which is indeed the choicer, the profounder, and politer method, to get a thorough insight into the index, by which the whole book is governed and turned, like fishes by the tail."

"When I am reading a book, whether wise or silly, it seems to me to be alive and talking to me."

"For Learning's mighty Treasures look
In that deep Grave a Book."

"There are the men who pretend to understand a book by scouting through the index: as if a traveler should go about to describe a palace when he had seen nothing but the privy."

"Books, the children of the brain."

"If men of wit and genius would resolve never to complain in their works of critics and detractors, the next age would not know that they ever had any."

A. J. A. SYMONS
1900–1941

". . . behind all the paraphernalia of bibliography, behind the bookshops, auctions, exhibitions, catalogues, collections and research which define the collector's efforts, is the single fact of the love of books."

FIAT LUX
TYPOGRAPHIC LIBRARY AND MUSEUM OF THE AMERICAN TYPE FOUNDERS COMPANY
FOUNDED 1908
BR

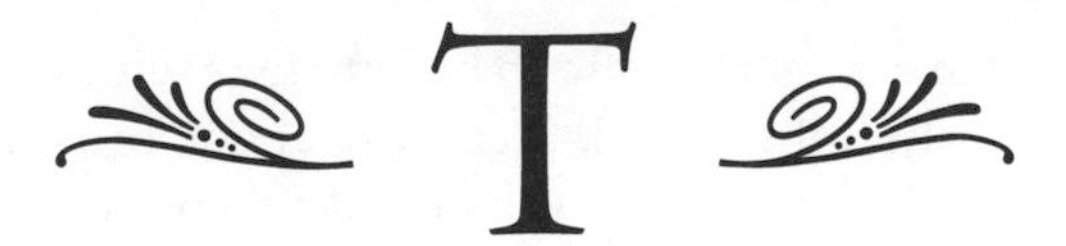

WILLIAM TARG
1907–

"To paraphrase James Joyce, 'I'm a man of small virtue,' inclined toward bibliomania and good writing. I'd be honored with the one-word epitaph, *Bookman*. My livelihood has been from making and selling books and serving as an obstetrician to authors. My private life has been, in large part, devoted to the acquisitive, namely, rare books and autograph material. I thank my stars for this hobby, this safety valve. It is, I believe, a much safer pursuit in the long run than, say, transient blondes, cards, booze, or horses. From childhood (when the gift of a few blocks of white notepaper would bring me pure joy), I had the bookman's passion. My destiny was obvious—to be a bookman."

"From a lifetime of involvement with words and writing, and from my own attempts at writing here, I've learned one fact: There Is No Such Thing as a Publishable First Draft. A strong back is the answer to good writing."

"One of the foremost rare-book dealers in the world . . . told me that if you put an intelligent, average dog into a bookshop, it would, in time, perhaps twenty years, learn almost everything one needs to know about the business of selling books."

"Book-collecting is one of the most gratifying, if inexhaustible, of all hobby-pursuits. All the pleasures (and pains) of angling are inherent in it; but unlike the angler who brays and boasts of catches mostly mythical, the book-fisher is able to *display* his catch as he boasts. His books are not cooked and consumed, nor do they wear out or disintegrate."

"Many authors should be shunned socially. Some are almost not human. There are perhaps no more than a dozen living authors I would care to know intimately, socially. I can't think of more than a dozen I'd care to be left alone with on a desert island. On the other hand, I can list about three hundred living authors whose works I would like to publish."

"[Is] there any excitement to compare with the opening of a fresh parcel of books?"

"A book collector has friends everywhere. The bookseller from whom you buy books is, more frequently than not, your friend. There is a bond between you that transcends the commercial transaction. For you've established *something* (call it rapport) between you that is personal, almost spiritual if you will. He understands your interests and your needs and the compulsion which brings you to him. (And let it be freely admitted, his magnet is as compelling to the bibliophile as the bar is to the boozer.) The bookseller becomes inextricably identified with you, your library, your intellectual life."

WILLIAM TEMPLE
1628–1699

"Books, like proverbs, receive their chief value from the stamp and esteem of ages through which they have passed."

ALFRED LORD TENNYSON
1809–1892

"I will bury myself in books, and the Devil may pipe to his own."

"Not with blinded eyesight poring over miserable books."

"For she was cramm'd with theories out of books."

"Oh! teach the orphan boy to read."

"I like those great *still* books. I wish there were a great novel in hundreds of volumes that I might go on and on. . . ."

"I can't read *Ben Jonson*, especially his comedies. To me he appears to move in a wide sea of glue."

TERENCE
190?–159? B.C.

"The fate of books depends on the capacity of the reader."

WILLIAM M. THACKERAY
1811–1863

"If a secret history of books could be written, and the author's private thoughts and meanings noted down alongside of his story, how many insipid volumes would become interesting, and dull tales excite the reader."

"Novelists are supposed to know everything, even the secrets of female hearts, which the owners themselves do not perhaps know."

"Fiction carries a greater amount of truth in solution than the volume which purports to be all true."

DYLAN THOMAS
1914–1953

"Persons with manners do not read at table."

ISAIAH THOMAS
1749–1831

"Printing removed the veil which obscured the reason of man; it broke the chain that bound him in superstition. By multiplying copies of the labors of the learned, and dispersing those copies over the earth, even to its remotest regions, he was enabled to search after truth in religion, in philosophy, in politics; and improvement in the mechanic arts."

"The press had become free some years previous to the commencement of the revolution; but it continued for a long time duly to discriminate between liberty and licentiousness. This freedom of the press was the first, and one of the greatest agents in producing our national independence. The press appears to be now under no particular restraints, and no one can wish the liberty of it to be greater."

JAMES THOMSON
1700–1748

"Give a man a pipe he can smoke,
  Give a man a book he can read:
And his home is bright with a calm delight,
  Though the room be poor indeed."

HENRY DAVID THOREAU
1817–1862

"I never read a novel, they have so little real life and thought in them."

"I now have a library of nearly nine hundred volumes, over seven hundred of which I wrote myself."

"Blessed are they who never read a newspaper, for they shall see Nature, and through her, God."

". . . a truly good book is something as natural, and as unexpectedly and unaccountably fair and perfect, as a wild flower discovered on the prairies of the West or in the jungles of the East."

"A truly good book teaches me better than to read it. I must soon lay it down, and commence living on its hint. . . . What I began by reading, I must finish by acting."

"However much we may admire the orator's burst of eloquence, the noblest written words are as far above the fleeting spoken language as the firmament with its stars is behind the clouds."

"How many a man has dated a new era in his life from the reading of a book."

"To read well, that is, to read true books in a true spirit, is a noble exercise."

"Most men have learned to read to serve a paltry convenience . . . but of reading as a noble intellectual exercise they know little or nothing."

"Books are the treasured wealth of the world, the fit inheritance of generations and nations."

"Read the best books first, or you may not have a chance to read them at all."

"Homeliness is almost as great a merit in a book as in a house, if the reader would abide there."

JAMES THURBER
1894–1961

"Mosher came out into the reception room, looking like a professor of English literature who has not approved of the writings of anybody since Sir Thomas Browne."

"With sixty staring me in the face, I have developed inflammation of the sentence structure and a definite hardening of the paragraphs."

"Some American writers who have known each other for years, have never met in the daytime or when both were sober."

JOHN TODHUNTER
1839–1916

"Man walks the earth
The quintessence of dust:
Books, from the ashes of his mirth
Madness and sorrow, seem
To draw the elixir of some rarer gust;
Or, like the Stone of Alchemy, transmute
Life's cheating dross to golden truth of
dream.

ALVIN TOFFLER
1928–

"The expansion of knowledge implies that each book . . . contains a progressively smaller fraction of all that is known."

LEO TOLSTOY
1828–1910

"Instead of going to Paris to attend lectures, go to the public library, and you won't come out for twenty years, if you really wish to learn."

"Three times in my life I have read through Shakespeare and Goethe from end to end. And I never could make out in which their charm consisted."

"In a writer there must always be two people—the writer and the critic."

H. M. TOMLINSON
1873–1958

"The good book is always a book of travel; it is about a life's journey."

"It has to be a good book which can maintain its value beside the lamp of a ship's berth at midnight—the best time and place in all the world for reading."

ARNOLD TOYNBEE
1889–1975

"The student, when he enters one of the great bookshops in his university town, is learning the extremely important part of educating himself. Browsing in a bookshop teaches him to explore the wide world of literature, and to do this on his own initiatives without guidance. He is learning to find his way for himself and finding his way for himself is one of the most important parts of education."

G. M. TREVELYAN
1876–1962

"Education . . . has produced a vast population able to read but unable to distinguish what is worth reading."

ANTHONY TROLLOPE
1815–1882

"The habit of reading is the only enjoyment in which there is no alloy; it lasts when all other pleasures fade."

"Let biographers, novelists, and the rest of us groan as we may under the burdens which we so often feel too heavy for our shoulders; we must either bear them up like men, or own ourselves too weak for the work we have undertaken."

"The end of a novel, like the end of a children's dinner party, must be made up of sweetmeats and sugar-plums."

"There is no way of writing well and also of writing easily."

"The one most essential obstacle to the chance of success was probably Lady Carbury's conviction that her end was to be obtained not by producing good books, but by inducing certain people to say that her books were good."

"Of all the needs a book has the chief need is that it be readable."

"Three hours a day will produce as much as a man ought to write."

"If indeed a man writes his books badly, or paints his pictures badly, because he can make his money faster in that fashion than by doing them well, and at the same time proclaims them to be the best he can do,—if in fact he sells shoddy for broadcloth,—he is dishonest, as is any other fraudulent dealer."

"That I can read and be happy while I am reading, is a great blessing. Could I remember, as some men do, what I read, I should have been able to call myself an educated man. But that power I never possessed. Something is always left,—something dim and inaccurate,—but still something sufficient to preserve the taste for more."

"I was once told that the surest aid to the writing of a book was a piece of cobbler's wax on my chair. I certainly believe in the cobbler's wax much more than the inspiration."

"Is it not singular how some men continue to obtain the reputation of popular authorship without adding a word to the literature of their country worthy of note? . . . To puff and to get one's self puffed have become different branches of a new profession."

"Let an author so tell his tale as to touch his reader's heart and draw his tears and he has, so far, done his work well."

"There should be no episodes in novels."

"[Novelists] are the great instructors of the country. They help the Church and are better than the Law. They teach ladies to be women, and they teach men to be gentlemen."

FRANCES TROLLOPE
1780–1863

"The character of the American literature is, generally speaking, pretty justly appreciated in Europe. The immense exhalation of periodical trash, which penetrates into every cot and corner of the country, and which is greedily sucked in by all ranks, is unquestionably one great cause of its inferiority."

SOJOURNER TRUTH
1797?–1883

"I . . . can't read a book but I can read the people."

BARBARA TUCHMAN
1912–1989

"Books are the carriers of civilization. Without books, history is silent, literature dumb, science crippled, thought and speculation at a standstill. They are engines of change, windows on the world, 'lighthouses' as a poet said 'erected in the sea of time.' "

MARTIN F. TUPPER
1810–1889

"A good book is the best of friends, the same to-day and forever."

ANNE TYLER
1941–

"I think I was born with the impression that what happened in books was much more reasonable, and interesting, and *real*, in some ways than what happened in life."

"I write because I want more than one life; I insist on a wider selection. It's greed plain and simple. When my characters join the circus, I'm joining the circus. Although I'm happily married, I spend a great deal of time mentally living with incompatible husbands."

ROYALL TYLER
1757–1826

"The bookworm's features scrawl a smile
While gloating on the musty page,
As we admire some ruined pile,
Not for its worth, but for its age.

The sprawling letters, yellow text,
The formal phrase, the bald stiff style,
The spelling quaint, the sense perplext,
Provoke his unaccustomed smile.
Like Kennicot he cites and quotes,
On illustration clear intent;
And in the margin gravely notes
A thousand meanings—never meant."

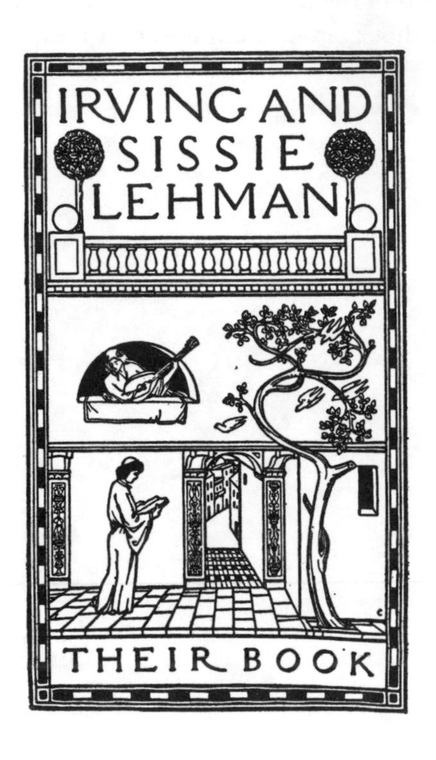
IRVING AND
SISSIE
LEHMAN
THEIR BOOK

STANLEY UNWIN
1884–1968

"Your book may be a masterpiece but do not suggest that to the publisher because many of the most hopeless manuscripts that have come his way have probably been so described by their authors."

"Another illusion, seldom entertained by competent authors, is that the publisher's readers and others are waiting to plagiarize their work. I think it may be said that the more worthless the manuscript, the greater the fear of plagiarism."

JOHN UPDIKE
1932–

"When I write, I aim in my mind not toward New York but toward a vague spot a little east of Kansas. I think of the books on library shelves, without their jackets, years old, and a countryish teenaged boy finding them, and having them speak to him. The reviews, the stacks in Brentano's, are just hurdles to get over, to place the books on that shelf."

PETER USTINOV
1921–

"Books, I don't know what you see in them. . . . I can understand a person reading them, but I can't for the life of me see why people have to write them."

OCTAVE UZANNE
1852–1931

"To turn over the pages of a book long coveted, to handle an unexpected find, to fondle a binding, to dust the edges, are exquisite joys in which the hand shares with the eye."

V

JOHN VANBRUGH
1664–1726

"For to mind the inside of a book, is to entertain one's self with the forced product of another man's brain. Now I think a man of quality and breeding may be much better diverted with the natural sprouts of his own."

MARK VAN DOREN
1894–1973

"The art of reading is among other things the art of adopting that pace the author has set. Some books are fast and some are slow, but no book can be understood if it is taken at the wrong speed."

VINCENT VAN GOGH
1853–1890

"I think that I still have it in my heart someday to paint a bookshop with the front yellow and pink, in the evening, and the black passerby . . . like a light in the midst of darkness."

LUC DE CLAPIER VAUVENARGUES
1715–1747

"In a way, the main fault of all books is that they are too long."

FIORENTIO VESPASIANO DA BISTICCI
1421–1498

"In that library [the Duke of Urbino's] the books are all beautiful in a superlative degree, and all written by the pen. There is not a single one of them printed, for it would have been a shame to have one of that sort."

GORE VIDAL
1915–

"I never went to college. But I have lectured on campuses for a quarter-century, and it is my impression that after taking a course in The Novel, it is an unusual student who would ever want to read a novel again."

"In America, the race goes to the loud, the solemn, the hustler. If you think you're a great writer, you must say that you are."

"Ideally, the writer needs no audience other than the few who understand. It is immodest and greedy to want more."

"It is not the novel that is declining, but the audience for it."

"I read a good deal of criticism, but only as a vice, not so good as reading science fiction, rather better than reading mystery stories."

VOLTAIRE
1694–1778

"Books rule the world, at least those nations which have a written language. The others do not count."

"The multitude of books is making us ignorant."

"It is far better to be silent than merely to increase the quantity of bad books."

"What harm can a book do that costs a hundred crowns? Twenty volumes folio will never cause a revolution; it is the little portable volumes of thirty cents that are to be feared."

"It is with books as with men: a very small number play a great part, the rest are lost in the multitude."

"A man may be a very good author with some faults, but not with many faults."

"History is the recital of facts represented as true. Fable, on the other hand, is the recital of facts represented as fiction."

ELIZABETH VON ARNIM
1866–1941

"The way Frederick made his living was one of the standing distresses of her life. He wrote immensely popular memoirs regularly, every year, of the mistresses of kings. There were in history numerous kings who had had mistresses, and there were still more numerous mistresses who had had kings; so that he had been able to publish a book of memoirs during each year of his married life, and even so there were great further piles of these ladies waiting to be dealt with."

"I hate authors. I wouldn't mind them so much if they didn't write books."

"For a person who wrote books, thought Rose, Frederick didn't seem to have much imagination."

KURT VONNEGUT, JR.
1922–

"Writers can treat their mental illnesses every day."

"I have long felt that any reviewer who expresses rage and loathing for a novel is preposterous. He or she is like a person who has put on full armor and attacked a hot fudge sundae or a banana split."

"My relatives say that they are glad I'm rich, but that they simply cannot read me."

"There is no shortage of wonderful writers. What we lack is a dependable mass of readers. . . . I propose that every person out of work be required to submit a book report before he or she gets his or her welfare check."

MARY HEATON VORSE
1881–1966

"The art of writing is the art of applying the seat of the pants to the seat of the chair."

Ex·Libris·
JoHN-JAY
FARNSWoRTH

DIANE WAKOSKI
1937–

"I write in the first person because I have always wanted to make my life more interesting than it was."

ALICE WALKER
1944–

"Deliver me from writers who say the way they live doesn't matter. I'm not sure a bad person can write a good book. If art doesn't make us better, then what on earth is it for?"

"I've been in . . . another college . . . a college of books—musty old books that went out of print years ago."

MARGARET WALKER
1915–

"When I was about eight, I decided that the most wonderful thing, next to a human being, was a book."

HORACE WALPOLE
1717–1797

"The sums laid out on books one should, at first sight, think an encouragement to letters; but booksellers only are encouraged, not books."

"What a pity it is I was not born in the golden age of Louis the Fourteenth, when it was not only the fashion to write folios, but to read them too."

"Without grace no book can live, and with it the poorest may have its life prolonged."

"When men write for profit, they are not very delicate."

"I have always rather tried to escape the acquaintance and conversation of authors. An author talking of his own works, or censuring those of others, is to me a dose of ipecacuana."

"I write I neither know how nor why, and always make worse when I try to amend."

"I am persuaded that foolish writers and readers are created for each other; and that Fortune provides readers as she does mates for ugly women."

HUGH WALPOLE
1884–1941

"A bibliomaniac is one to whom books are like bottles of whiskey to the inebriate, to whom anything that is between covers has an intoxicating savor."

EUGENE FITCH WARE
1841–1911

"Man builds no structure which outlives a book."

CHARLES DUDLEY WARNER
1829–1900

"Nothing is worth reading that does not require an alert mind."

"Have you any right to read, especially novels, until you have exhausted the best part of the day in some employment that is called practical?"

ROBERT PENN WARREN
1905–1989

"Your business as a writer is not to illustrate virtue but to show how a fellow may move toward it or away from it."

BOOKER T. WASHINGTON
1856–1915

"From the time that I can remember having any thoughts about anything, I can recall that I had an intense longing to learn to read. I determined, when quite a small child, that, if

I accomplished nothing else in life, I would in some way get enough education to enable me to read common books and newspapers."

"I began at once to devour this book, and I think that it was the first one I ever had in my hands. I had learned from somebody that the way to begin to read was to learn the alphabet, so I tried in all the ways I could think of to learn it,—all of course without a teacher, for I could find no one to teach me. At that time there was not a single member of my race anywhere near us who could read, and I was too timid to approach any of the white people. In some way, within a few weeks, I mastered the greater portion of the alphabet."

"Mrs. Ruffner always encouraged and sympathized with me in all my efforts to get an education. It was while living with her that I began to get together my first library. I secured a dry-goods box, knocked out one side of it, put some shelves in it, and began putting into it every kind of book that I could get my hands upon, and called it my 'library.' "

GEORGE WASHINGTON
1732–1799

"I conceive that a knowledge of books is the basis on which all other knowledge rests."

ISAAC WATTS
1674–1748

"By reading of books, we may learn something, from all parts, of mankind."

EVELYN WAUGH
1903–1966

"Lady Peabury was in the morning room reading a novel; early training gave a guilty spice to this recreation, for she had been brought up to believe that to read a novel before luncheon was one of the gravest sins it was possible for a gentlewoman to commit."

"The best sort of book to start with is biography. If you want to make a success of it, choose as a subject someone very famous who has had plenty of books written about him quite recently. Many young writers make the mistake of choosing some forgotten Caroline clergyman or eighteenth-century traveller."

"Most writers in the course of their careers become thick-skinned and learn to accept vituperation, which in any other profession would be unimaginably offensive, as a healthy counterpoise to unintelligent praise."

"I never could understand how two men can write a book together; to me that's like three people getting together to have a baby."

"I have come to the conclusion that there is no such thing as normality. That is what makes story-telling such an absorbing task, the attempt to reduce to order the anarchic raw materials of life."

JOHN WEBSTER
1580?–1625?

"Ignorant asses visit stationers' shops, their use is not to inquire for good books, but new books."

MASON LOCKE WEEMS
1759–1859

"Humanity and Patriotism both cry aloud for Books, Books, Books."

SIMONE WEIL
1909–1943

"When literature becomes deliberately indifferent to the opposition of good and evil it betrays its function and forfeits all claim to excellence."

FAY WELDON
1931–

"Fortunately, there is more to life than death. There is for one thing, fiction. A thousand thousand characters to be sent marching out into the world to divert time from its forward gallop to the terrible horizon."

ARTHUR WELLESLEY, DUKE OF WELLINGTON
1769–1852

"In my situation as Chancellor of the University of Oxford, I have been much exposed to authors."

CAROLYN WELLS
1869–1942

"They borrow books they will not buy,
They have no ethics or religion;
I wish some kind Burbankian guy
Would cross my books with homing pigeons."

H. G. WELLS
1866–1946

"Good books are the warehouses of ideas."

EUDORA WELTY
1909–

"What discoveries I've made in the course of writing stories, all begin with the particular, never the general."

"I learned from the age of two or three that any room in our house, at any time of day, was there to read in, or to be read to."

"It had been startling and disappointing to me to find out that story books had been written by *people*, that books were not natural wonders, coming up of themselves like grass."

"Ever since I was first read to, then started reading to myself, there has never been a line read that I didn't *hear*. As my eyes followed the sentence, a voice was saying it silently to me. It isn't my mother's voice, or the voice of any person I can identify, certainly not my own. It is human, but inward, and it is inwardly that I listen to it. It is to me the voice of the story or the poem itself."

FRANZ WERFEL
1890–1945

"The true bibliophile loves the existence of a book more than its form and content; under no circumstances must he read it (is not something similar true of every great love?)."

JOHN WESLEY
1703–1791

"Read the most useful books, and that regularly, and constantly. Steadily spend all the morning in this employ, or, at least, five hours in four-and-twenty."

"Beware you be not swallowed up in books! An ounce of love is worth a pound of knowledge."

JESSAMYN WEST
1905–1984

"Writing is so difficult that I often feel that writers, having had their hell on earth, will escape punishment hereafter."

"Fiction reveals truths that reality obscures."

REBECCA WEST
1892–1983

"God forbid that any book should be banned. The practice is as indefensible as infanticide."

"Writers write for themselves and not for their readers. Art has nothing to do with communication between person and person, only with communication between different parts of a person's mind."

"Just how difficult it is to write biography can be reckoned by anybody who sits down and considers just how many people know the real truth about his or her love affairs."

EDITH WHARTON
1862–1937

"I was never allowed to read the popular American children's books of my day because, as my mother said, the children spoke bad English *without the author's knowing it.*"

"In any really good subject, one only has to probe deep enough to come to tears."

BENJAMIN IDE WHEELER
1854–1927

"Give me a library, and I'll build a university about it."

EDWIN P. WHIPPLE
1819–1886

"Books are lighthouses erected in the great sea of time."

"Good books are the most precious of blessings to a people; bad books are among the worst of curses."

E. B. WHITE
1899–1985

"Reading is the work of the alert mind, is demanding, and under ideal conditions produces finally a sort of ecstasy. This gives the experience of reading a sublimity and power unequalled by any other form of communication."

"If we should ever inaugurate a hall of fame, it would be reserved exclusively and hopefully for authors who, having written four best-sellers, *still refrained* from starting out on a lecture tour."

ALFRED NORTH WHITEHEAD
1861–1947

"A man really writes for an audience of about ten persons. Of course if others like it, that is clear gain. But if those ten are satisfied, he is content."

RICHARD WHITLOCK
1616?–1672?

"Books are life's best business: vocation to these hath more emolument coming in, than all the other busy terms of life."

WALT WHITMAN
1819–1892

"Camarado, this is no book,
Who touches this touches a man."

"Books are to be called for and supplied on the assumption that the process of reading is not half-asleep, but in the highest sense an exercise, a gymnastic struggle; that the reader is doing something for himself. . . ."

"Shut not your doors to me proud libraries,
For that which was lacking on all your well-fill'd shelves yet needed most, I bring
Forth from the war emerging, a book I have made
The words of my book nothing, the drift of it every thing.
A book separate, not link'd with the rest nor felt by the intellect,
But you ye untold latencies will thrill to every page."

"Then falter not, O book, fulfil your destiny,
You not a reminiscence of the land alone,
You too as a lone bark cleaving the ether, purpos'd."

"Our fundamental want today in the United States is of a class, and the clear idea of a class, of native authors, literatures, far different, far higher in grade, than any yet known, sacerdotal, modern, fit to cope with our occasions, lands, permeating the whole mass of American mentality, taste, belief, breathing into it a new breath of life, giving it decision."

"Damn the expurgated books! I say damn 'em. The dirtiest book in all the world is an expurgated book."

CHRISTOPH MARTIN WIELAND
1733–1813

"Busy readers are seldom good readers. He who would read with pleasure and profit should have nothing else to do or to think of."

ELIE WIESEL
1928–

"One written sentence is worth 800 hours of film."

OSCAR WILDE
1856–1900

"I never travel without my diary. One should always have something sensational to read in the train."

"If one cannot enjoy reading a book over and over again, there is no use in reading it at all."

"More than half of modern culture depends on what one shouldn't read."

" 'What are American dry-goods?' 'American novels.' "

"Poets know how useful passion is for publication. A broken heart will run to many editions."

"There is no such thing as an immoral book. Books are well written, or badly written."

"Mr. Henry James writes fiction as if it were a painful duty."

"The difference between journalism and literature is that journalism is unreadable and literature is not read."

"The play was a great success. But the audience was a failure."

"Anyone can make history. Only a great man can write it."

"In old days books were written by men of letters and read by the public. Nowadays books are written by the public and read by nobody."

"You should study the Peerage, Gerald. . . . It is the best thing in fiction the English have done."

"Of all peoples in the world the English have the least sense of literature."

"The one duty we have to history is to rewrite it."

"A poet can survive everything but a misprint."

"One must have a heart of stone to read the death of Little Nell without laughing."

IOLO A. WILLIAMS
1890–1962

"There collectors so foolish that they will not buy a book at all unless they are asked a good stiff price for it."

"In spite of folly, vulgarity and extravagance, the collecting of books is a pursuit for sane people. Its heart is sound, and its very blood is the record of man's achievement in the conquest of knowledge."

TENNESSEE WILLIAMS
1911–1983

"Literature has taken a back seat to the television, don't you think? It really has. We don't have a culture anymore that favors the creation of writers, or supports them very well."

WILLIAM CARLOS WILLIAMS
1883–1963

"For God's sake, make books that will fit an ordinary library shelf."

"I have never been one to write by rule, not even by my own rules."

ROBERT M. WILLIAMSON
B. 1851

"The bookseller who understands his business never shows any anxiety to sell his treasures; he acts as if it were a matter of perfect indifference to him whether he sells his books or not. His chief aim is to make his visitors feel at home in his shop, and having induced the customers to look at his wares, he leaves the books themselves to complete the transactions."

"It is not in keeping with his profession for a bookseller to be too young; or if he has the misfortune to be young he should appear old, and be antique in his conversation and ways."

"The pleasure of benefiting humanity is a pleasure the bookseller possesses in no small degree. In purchasing books from people who are weary of them, or have no further use for them, he rescues literature from lying idly aside, or from being destroyed by moths or damp; and in re-selling these books to fresh readers, he gives forgotten authors a new lease of life, helps to keep the immortal spirit of learning alive, and gives anew to men the delights of knowing the great minds of the past."

"As old age draws near, the man who has found his delight in athletic sports is unable to indulge his taste, but the lover of books can find a solace and joy in the companionship of his silent friends which increase as the years go round."

"There is a delight in just being in the presence of old books; one feels at home in the best society; the smell of the old leather binding is good, the homely honest letterpress is better, but the carrying away in one's pocket the volume as one's very own is best of all."

"The influence of dealing in books may and should be all for good in helping to ennoble the character of the bookseller. It is invariably the best kind of people who buy books and who have them to sell. Holding converse day by day with men of a literary temperament, habitually handling, thinking about, talking about, and dipping into books must help to mould one's character in the highest and best sense."

"In all ages the greatest, best, and most lovable men have been lovers of books."

ROBERT ARIS WILLMOTT
1809–1863

"An affecting instance of the tenderness and the compensations of Learning is furnished by the old age of [Bishop] Ussher, when no spectacles could help his failing sight, and a book was dark except beneath the strongest light of the window. Hopeful and resigned he continued his task, following the sun from room to room through the house he lived in, until the shadows of the trees disappeared from the grass, and the day was gone. How strange and delightful must have been his feelings, when the sunbeam fell brilliantly upon some half-remembered passage, and thought after thought shone out from the misty words, like the features of a familiar landscape in a clearing fog."

ANGUS WILSON
1913–1991

"There can be few more unrewarding tasks for the educated man of curiosity than the routine duties of librarianship."

AUGUST WILSON
1945–

"I had the freedom to explore and develop my mind. I went to the library to read things I didn't know anything about. I read everything I wanted."

EDMUND WILSON
1895–1972

"In a sense, one can never read the book that the author originally wrote, and one can never read the same book twice."

WOODROW WILSON
1856–1924

"The man who reads everything is like the man who eats everything: He can digest nothing; and the penalty for cramming one's mind with other men's thoughts is to have no thoughts of one's own."

"I would never read a book if it were possible for me to talk half an hour with the man who wrote it."

JOHN T. WINTERICH
1891–1970

"It is, after all, the collector's own fault if he does not know what he is about. What he eats may be his doctor's business, what he drinks his government's; what he reads and what he collects is indubitably his own private affair. It is his, not his bookseller's, to reason why. The bookseller's function is to supply and to inform, to play the role of philosopher and of friend, rarely indeed the role of guide."

P. G. WODEHOUSE
1881–1975

"I could see by the way she sniffed that she was about to become critical. There had always been a strong strain of book-reviewer blood in her."

THOMAS WOLFE
1900–1938

"He read insanely, by the hundreds, the thousands, the ten thousands, yet he had no desire to be bookish; no one could describe this mad assault upon print as scholarly; a ravening appetite in him demanded that he read everything that had ever been written about human experience. He pictured himself as tearing the entrails from a book as from a fowl. At first, hovering over bookstalls, or walking at night among the vast piled shelves of the library, he would read, watch in hand, muttering to himself in triumph or anger at the timing of each page: 'Fifty seconds to do that one. Damn you, we'll see! You will, will you?'—and he would tear through the next page in twenty seconds."

GEORGE E. WOODBURY
1855–1930

"What holy cities are to nomadic tribes—a symbol of race and a bond of union—great books are to the wandering souls of men; they are the Meccas of the mind."

VIRGINIA WOOLF
1882–1941

"No book is born entire and uncrippled as it was conceived."

"Each sentence must have, at its heart, a little spark of fire, and this, whatever the risk, the novelist must pluck with his own hands from the blaze."

"The creative power which bubbles so pleasantly in beginning a new book quiets down after a time, and one goes on more steadily. Doubts creep in. Then one becomes resigned. Determination not to give in, and the sense of an impending shape keep one at it more than anything."

" 'The proper stuff of fiction' does not exist; everything is the proper stuff of fiction, every feeling, every thought; every quality of brain and spirit is drawn upon; no perception comes amiss."

"Fiction is like a spider's web, attached ever so lightly perhaps, but still attached to life at all four corners."

"The poet gives us his essence, but prose takes the mold of the body and mind entire."

"I have sometimes dreamt that when the Day of Judgment dawns and the great conquerors and lawyers and statesmen come to receive their awards—their crowns, their laurels, their names carved indelibly upon imperishable marble—the Almighty will turn to Peter and will say, not without a certain envy when He sees us coming with our books under our arms, 'Look, these need no reward. We have nothing to give them here. They have loved reading.' "

"I read the book of Job last night—I don't think God comes well out of it."

"Literature is strewn with the wreckage of men who have minded beyond reason the opinion of others."

"We can easily conjure up a picture which does service for the bookish man and raises a smile at his expense. We conceive a pale, attenuated figure in a dressing-gown, lost in speculation, unable to lift a kettle from the hob, or address a lady without blushing, ignorant of the daily news, though versed in the catalogues of the second-hand booksellers, in whose dark premises he spends the hours of sunlight."

"To write weekly, to write daily, to write shortly, to write for busy people catching trains in the morning or for tired people coming home in the evening, is a heartbreaking task for men who know good writing from bad."

WILLIAM WORDSWORTH
1770–1850

"Dreams, books, are each a world; and books, as we know,
Are a substantial world, both pure and good:
Round these, with tendrils strong as flesh and blood,
Our pastime and our happiness will grow."

"Never forget what I believe was observed to you by Coleridge, that every great and original writer, in proportion as he is great and original, must himself create the taste by which he is to be relished."

"Do your duty to yourself immediately; love Nature and Books; seek these and you will be happy; for virtuous friendship, and love, and knowledge of mankind must inevitably accompany these, all things thus ripening in their due season."

"Go forth, my little book! pursue thy way;
Go forth, and please the gentle and the good."

RICHARD WRIGHT
1908–1960

"As I read, my ears are opened to the magic of the spoken word."

LAWRENCE C. WROTH
1884–1970

"The instinct to collect, like the process of fermentation, cannot be put out of existence by legislation nor can it be deprived of its vitality by the frowns of those who are insensitive to its urge. As long as people collect and as long as there are books there will be book collectors."

GEORGE WYNDHAM
1863–1913

"I have a wife, a son, a home, six good hunters and a library of Romance literature. I mean to enjoy them. If I am wanted, I can be found."

EX LIBRIS
EHN
Kingsclere
EDWARD
MORTON

X

MALCOLM X
1925–1965

"My alma mater was books, a good library. . . . I could spend the rest of my life reading, just satisfying my curiosity."

XENOPHON
445–391 B.C.

"The boys [in Persia] attending the public schools, pass their time in learning justice; and say that they go for this purpose, as those with us say who go to learn to read."

HARRIET
HEAD
YULE
EX LIBRIS
Frederick
Garrison
Hall

WILLIAM BUTLER YEATS
1865–1939

"When you are old and gray and full of sleep,
And nodding by the fire, take down this book,
And slowly read, and dream of the soft look
Your eyes had once, and of their shadows deep."

ANZIA YEZIERSKA
1885–1970

"When I only begin to read, I forget I'm on this world. It lifts me on wings with high thoughts."

EDWARD YOUNG
1683–1765

"Who knows if Shakespeare might not have thought less, if he had read more?"

"Another writes because his father writ,
And proves himself a bastard by his wit."

"An author! 'tis a venerable name!
How few deserve it, and what numbers claim."

MARGUERITE YOURCENAR
1903–1987

"A young musician plays scales in his room, and only bores his family. A beginning writer, on the other hand, sometimes has the misfortune of getting into print."

Leila H. Cole,
Her Book

Z

EMILE ZOLA
1840–1902

"These are the decisive facts; as soon as people know how to read, and as soon as they can read cheaply, the publishers' business increases tenfold, and the writer finds a means of living by the work of his pen. For this reason he no longer seeks the protection of the great; parasiticism disappears from among us; an author is a workman like any other, and gains his livelihood by his work."

"It is childish nowadays to complain of the difficulty of approaching a publisher. They publish too much; the number of volumes which appear each year in France amounts to thousands. When you look at the trash, the mediocre books which lumber up the shelves, one asks one's self what books the publishers could possibly have refused."

"The weak ones in literature deserve no pity."

HOWARD ZINN
1922–

"If there were criminal penalties I might have been charged with 'assault with a deadly weapon—a book. . . .' "

STEFAN ZWEIG
1881–1942

"If I ask myself today when we found time to read all those books, crammed full as our days were with school and private lessons, it becomes clear to me that it was mostly at the expense of our sleep and therefore of our bodily vigor. Although I had to get up at seven, I never put down my book before one or two in the morning—the bad habit of reading for one or two hours no matter how late at night it may be has remained with me ever since."

"The minute arrived when, with bated breath, I read that the publisher had decided to publish my book and even stipulated an option for later ones. The package with the first set of proofs came and was untied in great excitement, so as to see the type, the type-page, the very embryo of the book, and then, after a few weeks, the book itself, the first copies. One never tired of looking at them, touching them, comparing them, again and again and again. And then the childish visits to the bookstores to see if copies were already on display, whether they were resplendent in the center of the shop or hidden bashfully at the side. And then to await the first letters, the first notices, the first reply from the unknown, the incalculable. I secretly envy the young man all his suspense, excitement and enthusiasm, who casts his first book into the world!"

[SELECTED BIBLIOGRAPHY]

THIS IS A LIST of some representative books on the subjects of book collecting, libraries, reading, the book arts, and authorship. The list is by no means exhaustive (Montaigne may well have been correct when he wrote, "There are more books upon books than upon all other subjects"); rather, the aim here is to provide readers with a starting point for pursuing their bibliophilic interests. For hundreds of additional related titles, check the subject catalogue of any good-sized library under "Book collecting," "Bibliomania," "Books and reading," "Reading," and "Libraries." Those whose biblioholic passion demands ownership rather than borrowing will find that regular visits to new and antiquarian bookstores provide both access to many of the volumes listed here and ample proof that, in Vincent Starrett's words, "When we are collecting books, we are collecting happiness."

Mortimer J. Adler, *How to Read a Book: The Art of Getting a Liberal Education* (New York, 1940).

Nicholas A. Basbanes, *A Gentle Madness: Bibliophiles, Bibliomanes, and the Eternal Passion for Books (New York, 1995).*

Paul A. Bennett, *Books and Printing: A Treasury for Typophiles* (Cleveland, 1951).

Otto L. Bettmann, *The Delights of Reading: Quotes, Notes & Anecdotes* (Boston, 1987).

Sven Birkerts, *The Gutenberg Elegies: The Fate of Reading in an Electronic Age* (Boston, 1994).

Stuart Brent, *The Seven Stairs* (1962; rpt. ed. New York, 1989).

Anatole Broyard, *Aroused by Books* (New York, 1974).

Eric Burns, *The Joy of Books: Confessions of a Lifelong Reader* (Amherst, N.Y., 1995).

John Hill Burton, *The Book-Hunter* (1895; rpt. ed., Detroit, 1970).

Richard de Bury, *The Love of Books* (London, 1907).

John Carter, *Books and Book-Collectors* (London, 1956).

———, *Taste & Technique in Book Collecting* (1948; rpt. ed., London, 1970).
Barton Wood Currie, *Fishers of Books* (Boston, 1931).
John Cotton Dana, *Libraries: Address and Essays* (White Plains, N.Y., 1916).
Thomas F. Dibdin, *The Bibliomania or Book-Madness* (Boston, 1903), 4 vols.
Gerald Donaldson, *Books: Their History, Art Power, Glory, Infamy, and Suffering According to Their Creators, Friends and Enemies* (New York, 1981).
Estelle Ellis, Caroline Seebohm & Christopher Simon Sykes, *At Home With Books: How Booklovers Live With and Care for Their Libraries* (New York, 1995).
Charles P. Everitt, *The Adventures of a Treasure Hunter: A Rare Bookman in Search of American History* (Boston, 1951).
Eugene Field, *The Love Affairs of a Bibliomaniac* (New York, 1896).
H. George Fletcher, ed., *A Miscellany for Bibliophiles* (New York, 1979).
Antonia Fraser, ed., *The Pleasure of Reading* (London, 1992).
R. S. Garnett, *Some Book-Hunting Adventures: A Diversion* (Edinburgh, 1931).
Charles E. Goodspeed, *Yankee Bookseller* (Boston, 1937).
W. Carew Hazlitt, *The Book-Collector* (London, 1904).
Harold S. Holmes, *Some Random Reminiscences of an Antiquarian Bookseller* (Oakland, Cal., 1967).
Salvatore J. Iacone, *The Pleasures of Book Collecting* (New York, 1976).
Alexander Ireland, ed., *The Book-Lover's Enchiridion* (1888; rpt. ed., Detroit, 1969).
Holbrook Jackson, *The Anatomy of Bibliomania* (New York, 1950).
———, *Bookman's Holiday: A Recreation for Book Lovers* (London, 1945).
John H. Jenkins, *Audubon, and Other Capers: Confessions of a Texas Bookmaker* (Austin, Tex., 1976).
John Kieran, *Books I Love* (Garden City, N.Y., 1969).
Theodore Wesley Koch, ed., *Tales for Bibliophiles* (Chicago, 1929).
H. P. Kraus, *A Rare Book Saga* (New York, 1978).
D. W. Krummel, comp., *A Librarian's Collacon* (Urbana, Ill., 1971).
Andrew Lang, *Books and Bookmen* (London, 1887).

William E. Lickfield, ed., *Owed to the Book* (Philadelphia, 1957).
Douglas C. McMurtrie, *The Book: The Story of Printing & Bookmaking* (1943; rpt. ed., New York, 1989).
Kathleen Molz, "The Librarian's Commonplace Book," *Wilson Library Bulletin*, 42 (1968): 980–1017.
Christopher Morley, comp., *Ex Libris* (New York, 1936).
William Morris, *The Ideal Book: Essays and Lectures on the Art of the Book* (Berkeley, Cal., 1982).
A. Edward Newton, *The Amenities of Book-Collecting and Kindred Affections* (Boston, 1918).
———, *This Book-Collecting Game* (Boston, 1928).
———, *A Magnificent Farce, and Other Diversions of a Book-Collector* (Boston, 1921).
John B. Nicholson, Jr., *Reading and the Art of Librarianship: Selected Essays* (New York, 1986).
William Dana Orcutt, *In Quest of the Perfect Book: Reminiscences and Reflections of a Bookman* (Boston, 1926).
———, *The Kingdom of Books* (Boston, 1927).
———, *The Magic of the Book: More Reminiscences and Adventures of a Bookman* (Boston, 1930).
Edmund L. Pearson, *The Librarian: Selections from the Column of That Name* (Metuchen, N.J., 1976).
Noel Perrin, *A Reader's Delight* (Hanover, N.H., 1988).
Jean Peters, ed., *Book Collecting: A Modern Guide* (New York, 1977).
———, ed., *Collecting Books: Some New Paths* (New York, 1979).
David Powell, comp., *The Wisdom of the Novel: A Dictionary of Quotations* (New York, 1985).
Lawrence Clark Powell, *The Alchemy of Books* (Los Angeles, 1954).
———, *Books in My Baggage: Adventures in Reading* (Cleveland, 1959).
———, *A Passion for Books* (Cleveland, 1958).
Claude A. Prance, *The Laughing Philosopher: A Further Miscellany on Books, Booksellers and Book Collecting* (London, 1976).
Tom Raabe, *Biblioholism: The Literary Addiction* (Golden, Co., 1991).
David A. Randall, *Dukedom Large Enough* (New York, 1969).
Gordon N. Ray, *Books as a Way of Life: Essays* (New York, 1988).
A. S. W. Rosenbach, *A Book Hunter's Holiday* (Boston, 1936).
———, *Books and Bidders: The Adventures of a Bibliophile* (Boston, 1927).

Leona Rostenberg & Madeleine B. Stern, *Between Boards: New Thoughts on Old Books* (Montclair, N.J., 1978).

———, *Old & Rare: Thirty Years in the Book Business* (New York, 1974).

Howard S. Ruddy, ed., *Book Lovers' Verse* (Indianapolis, 1899).

Joseph Spence, *Anecdotes, Observations and Characters of Books and Men* (1820; rpt. ed., Carbondale, Ill., 1964).

Vincent Starrett, *Books Alive: A Profane Chronicle of Literary Endeavor and Literary Misdemeanor* (New York, 1940).

———, *Books and Bipeds* (New York, 1947).

———, *Born in a Bookshop: Chapters from the Chicago Renascence* (Norman, Ok., 1965).

Meic Stephens, comp., *A Dictionary of Literary Quotations* (London, 1990).

William Targ, ed., *Bouillabaisse for Bibliophiles* (Cleveland, 1955).

———, ed., *Carrousel for Bibliophiles* (1947; rpt. ed., Metuchen, N.J., 1967).

———, *Indecent Pleasures: The Life and Colorful Times of William Targ* (New York, 1975).

Alan G. Thomas, *Great Books and Book Collectors* (New York, 1975).

James Thompson, comp., *Books: An Anthology* (Melbourne, 1968).

Robert M. Williamson, *Bits from an Old Book Shop* (London, 1904).

John T. Winterich & David A. Randall, *A Primer of Book Collecting* (1926; 3rd rev. ed., New York, 1966).

Louis B. Wright, *Of Books and Men* (Columbia, S.C., 1976).

[INDEX]

This index provides a basic guide to subjects and people mentioned in the quotations in this book. In an effort to keep the index to a manageable length, there are few broad entries ("books," for example, seems superfluous in a collection like this one). Pseudonyms and alternate names are listed here with "see" references to the name under which that author's quotations appear in this volume.

ONLY IN BOOKS
is typeset in Adobe Jenson, designed by Robert Slimbach
and released in 1996 as an Adobe Multiple Master typeface.
It is modeled after Nicolas Jenson's classic roman font of 1470,
considered perhaps the most beautiful ever designed,
and the superb early-sixteenth-century italics of
Ludovico degli Arrighi.

Slimbach's Jenson retains the grace and balance
so admired in Jenson's and Arrighi's fonts,
producing pages of understated elegance, clarity, and integrity
in keeping with the tradition of fine books
published by Madison House.

In addition, as a Multiple Master typeface,
Adobe Jenson gives the typographer
unprecedented control of the fonts' proportions, enabling
independent adjustment of optical size and weight
to optimize its beauty and readability
in display, text, and notes.

Only in Books
was designed, typeset, and produced by
Impressions Book and Journal Services, Inc.,
Madison, Wisconsin and Ann Arbor, Michigan.

Designed by William Kasdorf